STUPID
ANCIENT
HISTORY

Other Books by Leland Gregory

STUPID
ANCIENT
HISTORY

LELAND GREGORY

**Andrews McMeel
Publishing, LLC**
Kansas City • Sydney • London

Andrews McMeel Publishing, LLC
an Andrews McMeel Universal company
1130 Walnut Street, Kansas City, Missouri 64106

www.andrewsmcmeel.com

12 13 14 15 16 RR2 10 9 8 7 6 5 4 3 2 1

ISBN: 978-1-4494-2157-1

Library of Congress Control Number: 2012936747

ATTENTION: SCHOOLS AND BUSINESSES
Andrews McMeel books are available at quantity
discounts with bulk purchase for educational, business, or
sales promotional use. For information, please e-mail the
Andrews McMeel Publishing Special Sales Department:
specialsales@amuniversal.com

STUPID
ANCIENT
HISTORY

DEAD FIRST, NOT LAST

Some of the earliest Olympic events make synchronized swimming look about as sissified as, well, synchronized swimming. One such event was called the pancration, a mix of boxing, wrestling, and endurance that had virtually no rules. During the pancration in 564 b.c., Arrachion of Phigalia earned a place in the record books, not only because he won the bout but because he died trying. Arrachion of Phigalia's opponent, whose name is now forgotten, conceded the event because Arrachion had nearly beaten him to death. As Arrachion lay on the ground he was declared the winner by default, but he refused to stand and claim victory. Was it because he was exhausted, or overcome with the joy of victory, perhaps? No. It was because he was dead. Since the bout had already been decided Arrachion became the only dead person in history to win an Olympic event, making the pancration less a triathlon than a die-athlon.

TO FIGHT OFF ROMAN SHIPS IN 300 b.c.,
CARTHAGINIANS CATAPULTED LIVE SNAKES AT THEM.

NAME YOUR POISON

According to Appian's *Roman History*, Mithradates VI Eupator of Pontus in Asia Minor (134–63 B.C.) routinely took small doses of a specially prepared poison to help him develop a resistance should anyone try to poison him. He was so successful in building up an immunity to poison that when he tried to take his own life to escape the approaching Romans, the poison he took had no effect. (It did, however, kill his two daughters who also took it.) Instead he requested his Gaul bodyguard and friend, Bituitus, to kill him with a sword. Mithridate, named after Mithradates, is a concoction with as many as sixty-five ingredients and is used as an antidote for poisoning. The recipe was found in Mithradates's cabinet, written in his own hand, and was taken to Rome.

III

VERY STATUESQUE

Can you imagine someone taking a beautiful piece of white marble Greek statuary and painting it flesh tones, making its hair black or brown, coloring the clothing, or, if the statue was naked, painting in pubic hair? You would think that would be considered vulgar and uncouth, but that's what the Greeks did. Statues in ancient times weren't cold, bland white likenesses of gods, kings, and noblemen; they were colorfully painted, and no detail was left to the imagination. Even busts were painted—and statues of people's heads were, too!

THE ATHENIAN LAWMAKER DRACO DIED OF
SUFFOCATION WHEN HE WAS COMPLETELY COVERED BY
GIFTS OF CLOAKS SHOWERED UPON HIM BY GRATEFUL
CITIZENS AT AN AEGINA THEATER IN 620 B.C.

CLEO, WE HARDLY KNEW YA

No matter what the revisionists say, Cleopatra was not black—she wasn't even Egyptian. The Cleopatra I'm talking about—the one Elizabeth Taylor portrayed—was actually titled Cleopatra VII Thea Philopator (there were seven queens named Cleopatra). Cleo was part Greek, part Macedonian, and part Iranian. She ruled Egypt from Alexandria, which, other than its location, was not an Egyptian city at all. It would be like someone in the future deciding the head of state of South Africa in the 1910s to the 1960s was black because South Africa is part of Africa and Africans are dark-skinned—not taking into account that South Africa was part of Great Britain and therefore the country's leaders were British. You can bet Cleopatra didn't look like Elizabeth Taylor, either.

V

ACCORDING TO GREEK
HISTORIAN AND BIOGRAPHER
PLUTARCH, KING PYRRHUS
OF EPIRUS, FROM WHOM THE
TERM "PYRRHIC VICTORY" IS
DERIVED, DIED WHILE FIGHTING
IN THE STREETS OF ARGOS
IN 272 B.C. HIS DEATH CAME
ABOUT WHEN AN OLD WOMAN
THREW A ROOF TILE AT HIM.
HE WAS SO STUNNED AT THE
UNFORESEEN ATTACK THAT IT
GAVE AN ARGIVE SOLDIER THE
OPPORTUNITY TO KILL HIM.

MESSAGES
FROM THE PAST 1

When Pompeii was covered in pumice and ashes from the eruption of Mount Vesuvius (a.d. 79), the city became frozen in time. It was undisturbed until its accidental rediscovery in 1748. When archaeologists started sifting through the ashes they discovered thousands of inscriptions and graffiti all around the city. This led to the formation of an organization called the *Corpus Inscriptionum Latinarum* in 1853, which aimed to record every known Latin inscription in a collection by the same name. Here are some of the examples they've found in Pompeii. (Note: The number after the location in parentheses is the catalog number of the inscription—not the date—in volume 4 of the *Corpus Inscriptionum Latinarum*.)

- (Bar/brothel of Innulus and Papilio) 3932: "Weep, you girls. My penis has given you up. Now it penetrates men's behinds. Goodbye, wondrous femininity!"

- (House of the Citharist; below a drawing of a man with a large nose) 2375: "Amplicatus, I know that Icarus is buggering you. Salvius wrote this."

- (In the vestibule of the House of Cuspius Pansa) 8075: "The finances officer of the emperor Nero says this food is poison."

- (Near the rear entrance vestibule of the House of Menander) 8356: "At Nuceria, look for Novellia Primigenia near the Roman gate in the prostitute's district."

- And an early example of a still-popular type of graffiti—found on the exterior of the House of Menander, 8304: "Satura was here on September 3rd."

BURNING DOWN THE HOUSE

Of the Seven Wonders of the Ancient World only one is still standing—the Great Pyramid of Giza (all the others were destroyed by fire or earthquake). The Temple of Artemis in Ephesus burned to the ground in 356 B.C. when an arsonist, hoping his name would live forever for his destructive feat, put a torch to it. The arsonist was executed, and to make sure his wish of everlasting fame wouldn't come true, it was ordered that his name be stricken from all records and never mentioned again. But you know how people talk. Despite the best efforts of the Ephesian authorities, the man's name leaked out, and Herostratus, the arsonist, is remembered as one of the most notorious firebugs in history.

VIII

THE CAESAR SALAD WAS NOT
NAMED AFTER JULIUS CAESAR. IT
WAS NAMED FOR ITS CREATOR,
CAESAR CARDINI, AN ITALIAN
IMMIGRANT WHO OPERATED A
RESTAURANT IN SAN DIEGO AND
ONE IN TIJUANA TO AVOID THE
RESTRICTIONS OF PROHIBITION.
THE SALAD WAS CREATED,
ACCORDING TO HIS DAUGHTER
ROSA, ON JULY 4, 1924.

AN X-TRAORDINARY LETTER

The XXXs today used to signify kisses in love letters, text messages, and e-mails started out as a legal symbol and not a romantic one. An X was the sign of Saint Andrew (who died circa A.D. 65), one of the apostles (both he and his brother Peter were fishermen by trade, and Jesus called them to be his disciples by saying he would make them "fishers of men"). In the early days, when one signed their name using an "X" it was an indication that they were pledging in the name of Saint Andrew that they promised to fulfill the terms of the document they were signing. The "X" comes from the Greek letter *chi*, which is the first letter of the Greek word Χριστός, translated as "Christ." This is where we get the alternate word for Christmas, "Xmas," which some believe is an effort to take Christ out of Christmas. So signing a document with an "X" could also mean the signee was pledging his honesty upon the name of Christ.

TO SHOW THAT WHAT THEY WERE SIGNING WAS TRUTHFUL, PEOPLE IN THE MIDDLE AGES WOULD KISS THEIR SIGNATURES. THIS WAS CALLED "THE KISS OF TRUTH," AND IT'S WHERE WE GOT THE EXPRESSION "SEALED WITH A KISS."

X

A RIPE OLD AGE

We're all lucky to be living in the modern age because if you reached thirty years old in ancient history you would be considered old. This is a common misinterpretation of statistical data on how old people lived to be in the ancient world. Taking the ages people die and then "averaging" those numbers together to come up with a median life expectancy is how scientists calculate life span. So technically it's true that two hundred years ago the average life span in North America was thirty-five to forty, and two thousand years ago it was twenty to twenty-five. But most deaths occur in one of two stages: infancy and people over seventy-five. Increase the number of one and you decrease the number of the other—it's an average. In Roman times infant mortality rates were approximately 319 out of 1,000 births—so almost a third (and this is optimistic) of children died in infancy. Of course, other factors affected life expectancy: poor nutrition, bad water, diseases, war, famine, etc. So, basically, thirty wouldn't have been considered old as much as lucky. In the census records for A.D. 74, Pliny reported several people claiming to be more than a hundred years old; one even claimed to be 140. (Pliny, *Natural History* 7.164.)

CUT IT OUT

Julius Caesar was born by caesarian section and that's where the procedure gets its name, right? More than likely not. There's no record of the manner in which Caesar was delivered but it's highly unlikely that it was through such a drastic surgery. In early times an operation such as this was performed only if the mother had died during childbirth. Bindusara (320–272 B.C.), the second Mauryan Samrat (emperor) of India, is regarded as the first child born by surgery. His mother, Durdhara, wife of Chandragupta Maurya (founder of the Mauryan Empire), died of accidental poisoning when she was close to delivery and, upon finding his dead wife, Chandragupta cut the baby from her belly. (M. Srinivasachariar, *History of Classical Sanskrit Literature*, 3rd ed.) In ancient times this operation was never performed on a healthy mother, and Caesar's mom lived a long time after his birth. The name "caesarian" comes from the Latin word *caedere*, "to cut."

THE MOST CONVINCING PIECE OF EVIDENCE THAT CAESAR WASN'T BORN BY CAESARIAN SECTION IS THAT THE NAME CAESAR HAD ALREADY BEEN IN THE FAMILY FOR GENERATIONS.

DREAM A LITTLE DREAM OF ME

Artemidorus Daldianus, also known as Ephesius, was a professional diviner who lived in the second century. He is known for his five-volume work, *Oneirocritica* (*The Interpretation of Dreams*). The fifth book is a collection of "case histories" collected from festivals in Italy, Greece, and Asia Minor (now Turkey).

- "A man dreamed that he had a mouth with big, beautiful teeth in his rectum, and that through it he spoke, ate, and performed all the normal functions of a mouth. He was subsequently exiled from his homeland for making incautious statements. I have not included the reason, for the outcome was easily predictable." (5.68.)

- "A man dreamt that he had three penises. He was a slave at the time and was set free. He then had three names instead of one, since he acquired an additional two names from the man who had set him free." (5.91.)

BEARING FALSE WITNESS I

The Bible is filled with wonderful, uplifting, inspiring passages—so why do people often misquote them, misinterpret them, or attribute phrases to the Bible that aren't even there? Here are some examples:

"Do unto others as you would have them do unto you." This exact phrase is not in the Bible but there are verses that are similar. One of the Bible verses that most closely resembles this colloquialism is Matthew 7:12 (King James Version): "Therefore all things whatsoever ye would that men should do to you, do ye even so to them."

"Pride goeth before a fall." People use this when they want to chastise someone for being arrogant or headstrong. But Proverbs 16:18 (KJV) actually reads "Pride goeth before destruction, and an haughty spirit before a fall." So, in essence, if someone is acting superior by telling another person not to be arrogant, they're actually the ones heading for "a fall."

THAT'S A WRAP!

The Egyptians have been regarded through the centuries as having perfected the preservation of bodies through mummification. The brain was dissolved with special chemicals and then removed through the nose with metal hooks. The internal organs, such as the liver, lungs, stomach, and intestines, were removed and preserved in jars. (The heart, which was considered the spiritual center, remained in the body.) The corpse was then slathered in salt to dry (or buried in the sand until all the moisture was removed) then covered in resin and wrapped. (This, of course, is the shortened version of the process.) When archaeologists found mummies in such pristine condition they initially thought the Egyptians had discovered some amazing preservation techniques. But the primary reason the mummies held up as well as they did was because of the dryness of the climate, which resulted in a huge reduction in decomposition-causing bacteria. Human bodies also naturally mummify in extremely cold climates, when they are submerged in bogs (where air can't reach them), and in places with low humidity. In fact, animals that died naturally in the desert thousands of years ago were discovered to be as well preserved as Egypt's finest mummies, without all the fancy preparation.

STUPID
ANCIENT
HISTORY

BE IT EVER SO CRUMBLY, THERE'S NO PLACE LIKE ROME

Nero fiddled while Rome burned. Okay, first, if you're going to take this literally, the fiddle wasn't invented until the tenth century, so obviously this doesn't refer to Nero playing a hoedown while Rome roasted. "Fiddle" also means "to pass time aimlessly," so are we led to believe that Nero didn't do anything while Rome burned? According to Publius Cornelius Tacitus (A.D. 56–117), a senator and historian, in his book *Annals* (15.39), neither of these two accounts is true. Nero, or more formally Nero Claudius Caesar Drusus Germanicus (A.D. 37–68), was the Roman emperor from A.D. 54 to 68. According to Tacitus, Nero wasn't even in Rome when the "Great Fire" started on July 19, 64; he was in Anzio, about thirty-five miles south of Rome. When Nero heard of the fire he rushed back and directed the efforts to extinguish the blaze, which burned for six days, according to Tacitus. Nero opened shelters for the newly homeless, lowered the price of grain, and had food brought in from the rest of the empire to help feed the displaced, all of which he paid for out of his own pocket.

ROMAN CANDLE

Nero needed to blame someone for the fire so he blamed the newest rabble-rousers in Rome, the Christians. As Tacitus (*Annals* 15.44) tells us:

> Nero fastened the guilt and inflicted the most exquisite tortures on a class hated for their abominations, called Christians [or Chrestians] by the populace. . . . Mockery of every sort was added to their deaths. Covered with the skins of beasts, they were torn by dogs and perished, or were nailed to crosses, or were doomed to the flames and burnt, to serve as a nightly illumination, when daylight had expired.

So even though Nero never actually fiddled while Rome burned (nor did he ever feed Christians to the lions—there's no documentation to support that one), he obviously wasn't a very nice man.

THE ROMAN GODDESS JUNO RULES OVER
MARRIAGE, THE HEARTH, AND CHILDBIRTH,
HENCE THE POPULARITY OF JUNE WEDDINGS.

A Monumental Accomplishment

It's an image made popular by Hollywood: Thousands of slaves suffering through long hours in the hot sun, whipped until they fainted or fell dead at the feet of their overseer, forced to build the enormous pyramids of their pharaohs. This theory was proposed and propagated by Greek historians such as the "father of history," Herodotus (484–425 B.C.). It is a great story of miserable oppression and makes for some awesome scenes in epic movies, but it's not true. Archaeologists have discovered nearby worker's camps associated with construction at Giza that suggest it was built instead by tens of thousands of skilled workers. Miroslav Verner posited in his book *The Pyramids: Their Archaeology and History* that the labor was organized into a hierarchy, consisting of two "gangs" of one hundred thousand men, divided into five *zaa* or *phyle* of twenty thousand men each, broken down further into individual units based on the particular skills of the workers. These workers weren't slaves; they were local farmers and craftsmen, who volunteered to do the work and were paid—sort of an old-fashioned public works project.

THE EYES HAVE IT

"Eye for an eye, tooth for a tooth" is a proscription that is usually interpreted to mean harsh retribution for a crime—literally, if you injure my eye I get to injure your eye. This phrase is found in Hammurabi's code, section 230 (1792–1750 B.C.) and was made popular by Moses's injunction in both the Torah and the Bible around 500 B.C. (Exodus 21:24, Leviticus 24:20, and Deuteronomy 19:21; refuted by Jesus in Matthew 5:39 with "But I say unto you, That ye resist not evil: but whosoever shall smite thee on thy right cheek, turn to him the other also."). But the real meaning is better phrased, "Let the punishment meet the crime." In ancient times the measure of punishment was meted out by someone's standing in society. If, say, a slave stole a sheep he might be put to death—certainly not an "eye for an eye"(not even a ewe for a ewe), but a nobleman or landowner would receive a lesser penalty.

JULIUS CAESAR WAS NEVER CALLED THAT BY HIS COUNTRYMEN. HE WAS SIMPLY REFERRED TO AS "CAESAR." IN ROMAN DAYS A MAN WAS NOT CALLED BY HIS FIRST NAME UNLESS IT WAS NECESSARY TO DISTINGUISH HIM FROM HIS SIBLINGS.

A TOKEN OF OUR APPRECIATION

In October 1971 the Arbeia Roman Fort and Museum in South Shields in the United Kingdom was proudly displaying an exhibition of Roman artifacts found nearby (the museum is located near the end of Hadrian's Wall, built by the Romans around A.D. 160). One case contained a Roman sestertium coin identified by museum experts as having been minted sometime between A.D. 135 and 138.

But one visitor, nine-year-old Fiona Gordon, claimed to have seen similar coins much later than that given out as tokens by a local soda bottler. She pointed out the soda bottler's trademark on the reverse of the coin. The "R" museum officials had originally taken to mean "Roman" actually stood for the soft drink manufacturer—Robinson's. The realization they had been displaying a fake Roman coin made the curators feel like a gluteus maximus.

AT THE TIME OF GAIUS JULIUS CAESAR AUGUSTUS, ROME WAS SO DENSELY POPULATED THAT HE BANNED ALL WHEELED VEHICLES DURING THE DAYLIGHT HOURS.

MY, HOW TIME FLIES

Okay, here's something you might have thought about, or maybe not. Why do we count the years backward until we reach 1 B.C., and then start counting forward, but there's no year 0? Well, blame it on Dionysius Exiguus (A.D. 500–560) a monk born in Scythia Minor, which is the modern Dobruja shared by Romania and Bulgaria. He is credited with inventing *anno Domini* (abbreviated as AD or A.D.) and "before Christ" (abbreviated as BC or B.C.) used to label or number years used with the Julian and Gregorian calendars. Actually, at that time, the Western world operated under the Roman calendar, and the year we call A.D. 1 was known as the year 754. Dionysius took the only biblical reference to Jesus's birth—that he was born at the end of the reign of King Herod—and made an educated guess to start A.D. 1.

THE EGYPTIANS FED THEIR LABORERS A DIET CONSISTING OF RADISHES, GARLIC, AND ONIONS (AS PRIME INGREDIENTS, NOT THE WHOLE MEAL). THIS SOUNDS KIND OF NASTY UNTIL YOU REALIZE THAT THESE VEGETABLES ARE EXTREMELY RICH IN RAPHANIN, ALLICIN, AND ALLISTATIN. THE POWERFUL NATURAL ANTIBIOTICS WERE RESPONSIBLE FOR THE LACK OF DISEASE OFTEN ASSOCIATED WITH THE CLOSE QUARTERS OF THE WORK CAMPS.

ACTS TO DIE FOR I

The Bible and the Torah are filled with crimes worthy of death. In a lot of political and moral debate today, people like to pick and choose which abomination suits their particular platform and forget the rest. Here's a sampling of deadly acts:

- Anyone who dreams or prophesizes anything that is against God, or anyone who tries to turn you from God, is to be put to death. (Deuteronomy 13:5.)

- If anyone, even in your own family, suggests worshipping another god, kill them. (Deuteronomy 13:6–10.)

- If you find out a city worships a different god, destroy the city and kill all of its inhabitants . . . even the animals. (Deuteronomy 13:12–15.)

- Kill anyone with a different religion. (Deuteronomy 17:2–7)

- Any person who curseth his mother or father must be killed. (Leviticus 20:9.)

- Anyone who works on the seventh day, a Sabbath of rest to the Lord, shall be put to death. (Exodus 35:2.)

TOUCHÉ TURTLE

Aeschylus (525–456 B.C.) was a famous Greek playwright who is often referred to as "the father of tragedy." He might have received his nickname not because of the estimated seventy to ninety plays he wrote (of which only seven have survived), but by the way he is supposed to have died: tragically, of course. According to Pliny the Elder (A.D. 23–79), Aeschylus died when an eagle holding a tortoise in his talons flew over Aeschylus and, mistaking his bald head for a rock on which to break open the tortoise's shell, dropped the reptile on Aeschylus's skull, killing him (Aeschylus, and probably the tortoise, too). Here's Pliny's account:

> This eagle (the *morphnos*) has the instinct to break the shell of the tortoise by letting it fall from aloft, a circumstance which caused the death of the poet Aeschylus. An oracle, it is said, had predicted his death on that day by the fall of a house, upon which he took the precaution of trusting himself only under the canopy of the heavens. (Pliny, *Natural History* 10.3, "The Different Kinds of Eagles.")

MARRIAGE NIGHT-MARE

Attila the Hun was the feared leader of the Hunnic Empire from A.D. 434 until his death in 453. He had conquered parts of Europe by A.D. 450—his empire ran from the Caspian Sea to the edge of the Roman Empire, destroying villages and pillaging the countryside, and was one of the most feared enemies of the Western and Eastern Roman Empires. You would think that a warrior of his stature would have had an epic death, but he didn't. According to fifth-century Roman diplomat and Greek historian Priscus of Panium in his book *Byzantine History*, this is the story. Attila married a young woman named Ildico in A.D. 453 and celebrated with an enormous feast in honor of his marriage. He drank and gorged himself on food and then retired for the night with his new bride. During the night, Attila got a nosebleed and, being too inebriated to wake up, drowned in his own blood.

AN ALTERNATIVE THEORY, PROPOSED BY NIGEL MAN IN HIS BOOK *ATTILA*, IS THAT AFTER HEAVY DRINKING, ATTILA SUCCUMBED TO INTERNAL BLEEDING OR SUFFERED FROM A CONDITION CALLED ESOPHAGEAL VARICES, WHERE DILATED VEINS IN THE LOWER PART OF THE ESOPHAGUS RUPTURE, CAUSING MASSIVE HEMORRHAGING.

THE MUSICAL FRUIT

The Pythagoreans, followers of the Greek philosopher Pythagoras of Samos (570–495 B.C.), were well known during their time for their practice of the "Pythagorean diet" (which in the nineteenth century became known as vegetarianism). According to Plutarch's *De esu carn*, Pythagoreans not only refrained from meat but also refused to eat or even touch beans because of an adherence to metempsychosis, a belief wherein an individual incarnates from one body to another, either human, animal, or plant. They thought that beans had the potential for life because they looked like human genitalia or fetuses. However, Cicero, in his book *On Divination*, had a simpler reason why he believed the Pythagoreans didn't eat beans: because they caused flatulence.

ACCORDING TO LEGEND, ENEMIES OF PYTHAGORAS'S MOVEMENT SET FIRE TO HIS HOUSE, FORCING THE OLD MAN TO FLEE. HE NOTICED HE WAS ABOUT TO ENTER A BEAN FIELD AND STOPPED, DECLARING HE WOULD RATHER DIE THAN TOUCH BEANS. HIS ENEMIES SWOOPED IN AND QUICKLY SLIT HIS THROAT. (CHARLES SEIFE, ZERO: THE BIOGRAPHY OF A DANGEROUS IDEA, P. 38.)

MESSAGES FROM THE PAST II

Graffiti from Pompeii, collected and recorded in the *Corpus Inscriptionum Latinarum*. The number after the location in parentheses is the catalog number of the inscription (not the date) in volume 4:

- (Bar of Athictus; right of the door) 8442: "I screwed the barmaid."

- (Pottery shop or bar of Nicanor; right of the door) 10070: "Lesbianus, you defecate and you write, 'Hello, everyone!'"

- (Gladiator barracks) 8792: "On April 19th, I made bread."

- (Gladiator barracks) 8792b: "Antiochus hung out here with his girlfriend Cithera."

- (House of Pascius Hermes; left of the door) 7716: "To the one defecating here. Beware of the curse. If you look down on this curse, may you have an angry Jupiter for an enemy."

- (On the wall in the street) 8898: "Theophilus, don't perform oral sex on girls against the city wall like a dog."

- (House of Valerius Flaccus and Valerius Rufinus; right of the door) 4066: "Daphnus was here with his Felicla."

FLAUNTING HIS INTELLECT

Archimedes of Syracuse (287–212 B.C.) was a Greek mathematician, physicist, engineer, astronomer, and inventor of, among other things, the Archimedes screw (which transferred water up from a low-lying body of water). He was given the task by King Hiero II of finding out whether a crown he was given was made of pure gold, or if cheaper, less dense, metals were included—but he couldn't damage the crown in any way. One day while Archimedes was taking a bath he figured out how to solve the problem. According to Roman writer Marcus Vitruvius Pollio (70–15 B.C.), in his book *De architectura*, Archimedes had hit upon the idea of water displacement. Basically, the weight of an object displaced a certain amount of water when submerged, and Archimedes could therefore figure out if the crown was made of pure gold or not. He was so excited that he jumped out of his bathtub and into the streets shouting, "Eureka!" ("I have found it!"). He was so excited; in fact, he forgot to put on any clothes.

ARCHAEOLOGICAL EVIDENCE SHOWS THAT ANCIENT EGYPTIAN PHYSICIANS HAD POSSIBLY ADOPTED THEIR OWN VERSION OF THE HIPPOCRATIC OATH. ON THE TOMB OF NENKH-SEKHMET, CHIEF OF THE PHYSICIANS DURING THE FIFTH DYNASTY, THERE IS AN INSCRIPTION STATING "NEVER DID I DO EVIL TOWARD ANY PERSON."

PLINY, THE SEXIST

"Hailstorms, they say, whirlwinds, and lightning even, will be scared away by a woman uncovering her body while her monthly courses are upon her. The same, too, with all other kinds of tempestuous weather; and out at sea a storm may be lulled by a woman uncovering her body merely, even though not menstruating at the time. At any other time, also, if a woman strips herself naked while she is menstruating, and walks round a field of wheat, the caterpillars, worms, beetles, and other vermin will fall from off the ears of corn." (Pliny, *Natural History* 28.23.)

"On the approach of a woman in this state [on her period], meat will become sour, seeds which are touched by her become sterile, grasses wither away, garden-plants are withered up, and the fruit will fall from the tree beneath which she sits." (Pliny, *Natural History* 7.13.)

PERISHING PERSIAN

Mithridates was a young Persian soldier in the army of King Artaxerxes II and was sentenced to death by scaphism, which is pretty nasty. First, the person is strapped between two rowing boats (one inverted on top of the other), with their head, hands, and feet sticking out. They are then force-fed milk and honey until they contract diarrhea, their naked body is covered with more honey to attract insects, and they're left to float face up in the sun in a stagnant pond.

Here's an eyewitness account of the death of Mithridates:

> They then keep his face continually turned toward the sun; and it becomes completely covered up and hidden by the multitude of flies that settle on it. And as within the boats he does what those that eat and drink must needs do, creeping things and vermin spring out of the corruption and rottenness of the excrement, and these entering into the bowels of him, his body is consumed. When the man is manifestly dead, the uppermost boat being taken off, they find his flesh devoured, and swarms of such noisome creatures preying upon and, as it were, growing to his inwards. In this way Mithridates, after suffering for seventeen days, at last expired. (Lucius Mestrius Plutarchus, *Life of Artaxerxes.*)

A SLIGHT CHARACTER

The scholar and poet Philitas of Cos (340–285 B.C.) could be considered the world's first absentminded professor. So absentminded, in fact, that he routinely forgot to eat and grew incredibly thin and frail. It was reported by several sources that Philitas became so engrossed in his learning that he eventually died of malnutrition. Greek rhetorician and grammarian Athenaeus of Naucratis called him an academic so consumed by his studies that he wasted away and died (*Deipnosophistae* 23ab). Aelian, in *Varia historia* 9.14, reported: "They say that Philitas grew extremely thin. Thus as the slightest thing could easily send him sprawling, he put lead weights in his soles, so as not to be blown over if there happened to be a stiff wind."

ANCIENT EGYPTIAN PRIEST-DOCTORS USED MOLDY BREAD TO HELP CURE INFECTIONS THOUSANDS OF YEARS BEFORE THE DISCOVERY OF ANTIBIOTICS.

THE STOICAL LIFE

Chrysippus of Soli (279–206 B.C.) was a Greek Stoic philosopher. Stoicism is a form of philosophy that teaches that destructive emotions result from errors in logical reasoning and, therefore, an intellectually and morally perfect person would not suffer such emotions. Chrysippus, however, died in a most un-stoic way at age seventy-three. Diogenes Laërtius, in *Lives and Opinions of Eminent Philosophers*, gives two different accounts of the death of Chrysippus. One: "Chrysippus drank with open mouth some wine; Then became giddy, and so quickly died." And two, the more ironic death of a Stoic: "But some people say that he died of a fit of immoderate laughter. For that seeing his ass eating figs, he told his old woman to give the ass some unmixed wine to drink afterwards, and then laughed so violently that he died."

THE MOUSE THAT ROARED

During the Battle of Beth-zechariah in 162 B.C., between the Jewish Maccabees and Greek forces, Eleazar Avaran spotted a war elephant that he believed was carrying the Seleucid king Antiochus V. He rationalized that this particular elephant wore special armor and thus must be carrying a special person. The only weakness in the elephant's armor was at the underbelly, which, as one can surmise, is a very dangerous place to put oneself. But according to 1 Maccabees 6:43–46, Eleazar darted under the enormous elephant and thrust his spear into the animal's belly. The elephant died immediately, as did Eleazar when the elephant landed on him. Did this heroic act change the course of the battle? No, the smaller Jewish army was still defeated. Romano-Jewish historian Titus Flavius Josephus (A.D. 37–100) said that Eleazar did not gain any real effect from this daring act . . . other than making a name for himself.

XXXVI

THE GREEKS INVENTED AND USED A LOT OF THE SURGICAL EQUIPMENT RECOGNIZABLE TODAY, INCLUDING FORCEPS, SCALPELS, CATHETERS, AND SYRINGES FOR DRAWING PUS FROM WOUNDS. THE SURGEON KRITOBOULOS USED ONE UNIQUE INSTRUMENT, THE SPOON OF DIOCLES, TO REMOVE THE INJURED EYE OF PHILIP II OF MACEDON IN 354 B.C., WITHOUT UNDUE SCARRING.

THAT'S NO BULL

We've heard of cruel tortures such as waterboarding, forcing bamboo shoots under the fingernails, and the rack, among others, but the Greeks designed a torture device called the brazen bull and it gave new meaning to the phrase "hot foot." The device was created by metalworker Perillos of Athens around 540 B.C., and he proposed it to Phalaris, the tyrant of Acragas, Sicily, as a new means of executing criminals. Phalaris relates how Perillos sold him on the bull:

> When you are minded to punish any one, shut him up in this receptacle, apply these pipes to the nostrils of the bull, and order a fire to be kindled beneath. The occupant will shriek and roar in unremitting agony; and his cries will come to you through the pipes as the tenderest, most pathetic, most melodious of bellowings. Your victim will be punished, and you will enjoy the music. (*Phalaris* 1.)

Phalaris was so aghast at such a horrible device that he ordered Perillos into the bull to show how the screaming worked—then he had a fire set beneath the bull. Phalaris ordered his guards to remove Perillos before he toasted and then had him thrown off a cliff. But did Phalaris destroy the brazen bull? Nope, he used it on criminals and martyrs as it was intended.

MORE BULL

The Romans were recorded as having used the brazen bull to kill some Christians, most famously Saint Eustace, who was ordered roasted to death, along with his wife and sons, by Emperor Hadrian in A.D. 118. During the persecutions of Emperor Domitian in A.D. 92, Saint Antipas, bishop of Pergamum (first martyr in Asia Minor) was cooked to death in a brazen bull. Apparently this cruel device wasn't put out to pasture for a long time because nearly two centuries later, another Christian, Saint Pelagia of Tarsus, was sent to die in the belly of the bronze beast by Emperor Diocletian in A.D. 287.

SAINT EUSTACE WAS A LEGENDARY CHRISTIAN MARTYR WHO LIVED IN THE SECOND CENTURY A.D. BEFORE HE SAW A VISION OF JESUS BETWEEN THE ANTLERS OF A STAG DURING A HUNT IN TIVOLI NEAR ROME, PLACIDUS (HIS NAME BEFORE HIS CONVERSION) WAS A ROMAN GENERAL WHO SERVED THE EMPEROR TRAJAN.

MUMMY STUFF

The word "mummy" comes from the Arabic term *mumiyah*, meaning "embalmed body."

The oldest known naturally mummified humans were found in 1936 at the site named Inca Cueva No. 4 in South America. The two mummies and a mummified decapitated head were dated at six thousand years old.

The oldest known deliberate mummification is of a child (one of the Chinchorro mummies found in the Camarones Valley, Chile), and dates from around 5050 B.C.

The ancient Egyptians went mummy crazy and didn't just mummify people; cats, rams, and even the mummified body of an alligator have been found in various tombs.

THE TOMB OF PHARAOH
TUTANKHAMEN ("KING TUT")
WAS FOUND REMARKABLY
INTACT BY HOWARD CARTER
IN THE VALLEY OF THE KINGS IN
1923; IT CONTAINED NUMEROUS
TREASURES, INCLUDING
THE ROYAL TOILET SEAT.

Missed It by a Hair

Lucius Fabius Cilo, whose full name was Lucius Fabius Cilo Septiminus Catinius Acilianus Lepidus Fulcinianus, was a Roman senator of the second century A.D. Cilo was one of the richest and most influential men in Rome at the time. According to Pliny the Elder, Cilo became famous for being lactose intolerant—well, sort of. Pliny recounts that Cilo died by choking on "a single hair in a draught of milk." (*Natural History* 7.)

"ON THE RESTORATIVE POWERS OF MUSIC:
FLUTE MUSIC, WHEN PLAYED SKILLFULLY AND
MELODIOUSLY, WAS THOUGHT TO CURE SNAKEBITES."
(AULUS GELLIUS, *ATTIC NIGHTS* 4.13.)

CRAP OUT OF LUCK

Arius (A.D. 256–336) was an influential leader in the Christian congregation in Alexandria, Egypt, and attended the First Council of Nicaea, convened by Roman emperor Constantine in A.D. 325 (where leaders from the worldwide community of Christians gathered for the first time to agree on various dogmatic Christian principles). He's also known for having one of the first documented sh!t fits.

Greek Christian church historian Socrates of Constantinople, not to be confused with the Greek philosopher Socrates, described Arius's death in his book *Historia Ecclesiastica* as follows:

> A terror arising from the remorse of conscience seized Arius, and with the terror a violent relaxation of the bowels: he therefore enquired whether there was a convenient place near, and being directed to the back of Constantine's Forum, he hastened thither. Soon after a faintness came over him, and together with the evacuations his bowels protruded, followed by a copious hemorrhage, and the descent of the smaller intestines: moreover portions of his spleen and liver were brought off in the effusion of blood, so that he almost immediately died. The scene of this catastrophe still is shown at Constantinople, as I have said, behind the shambles in the colonnade: and by persons going by pointing the finger at the place, there is a perpetual remembrance preserved of this extraordinary kind of death.

SECRETS OF THE SPHINX

So who blew off the Sphinx's nose? The story has circulated for years that Napoléon's soldiers fired their bullets and cannonballs at the Great Sphinx of Giza and eventually shot its proboscis off. But there are sketches of the Sphinx by Danish naval captain and explorer Frederic Louis Norden, made in 1737 and published in 1755, illustrating the Sphinx already noseless—and that was before Napoléon was even born. Examination of the Sphinx's face shows that the nose was chiseled and pried off the face. (Mark Lehner, *The Complete Pyramids*, p. 4.)

The real culprit, according to Egyptian Arab historian al-Maqrizi (A.D. 1364–1442), in his book *al-Mawaiz wa al-'i'tibar bi dhikr al-khitat wa al-'athar* (1.333) was probably Sufi Muslim zealot Muhammad Sa'im al-Dahr, from the *khanqah* of Sa'id al-Su'ada. In A.D. 1378, Sa'im al-Dahr discovered Egyptian peasants making offerings to the Sphinx in the hope of increasing their harvest, and, becoming so swept up with religious indignation, he personally hacked away at the nose with a chisel and eventually pried it off the Sphinx's face.

NOT VERY HUMOROUS

When you went to a doctor in ancient Greek times, he wouldn't take your temperature—he might, however, take your blood or your phlegm, give you an enema, or induce vomiting. The Greeks believed that there were four "humors" making up the body, and an imbalance in these would lead to both mental and physical illnesses and ailments. All illnesses, they believed, were caused by either too much or too little of one or more of these humors, and it was their job to get you back in balance. The Four Humors, according to Theophrastus (371–287 B.C.), were:

- BLOOD: influences courage, hope, and love.

- YELLOW BILE: if in excess could lead to bad temper and anger.

- BLACK BILE: if it dominated the body would lead to sleeplessness and irritation.

- PHLEGM: responsible for rationality, but if depleted would dull the emotions.

Doctors would try to keep these humors in balance by bleeding, purging, and a whole plethora of gruesome procedures. It sounds like some crazy barbaric quackery, but the theory of humors was practiced well into the nineteenth century. Makes one's blood run cold, doesn't it?

MESSAGES
FROM THE PAST III

Graffiti from Pompeii, collected and recorded in the *Corpus Inscriptionum Latinarum*. The number after the location in parentheses is the catalog number of the inscription (not the date) in volume 4:

- (House of Cosmus and Epidia; right of the door) 6702: "Aufidius was here. Good-bye."

- (Just outside the Vesuvius Gate) 6641: "Defecator, may everything turn out okay so that you can leave this place."

- (Near the Vesuvius Gate) 7086: "Marcus loves Spendusa."

- (Barracks of the Julio-Claudian gladiators; column in the peristyle) 4289: "Celadus the Thracian gladiator is the delight of all the girls."

- (On the Street of Mercury) 1321: "Publius Comicius Restitutus stood right here with his brother."

- (Casa Vico degli Scienziati) 3042: "Cruel Lalagus, why do you not love me?"

- (House of Orpheus) 4523: "I have buggered men."

- (Woodworking Shop of Potitus) 3498: "What a lot of tricks you use to deceive, innkeeper. You sell water but drink unmixed wine."

MEDICINAL MUMMY

There's an odd rumor floating around that ground-up mummies were used in pharmaceuticals. This one's so weird it has to be true, and it is. In fact, in the Middle Ages, thousands of Egyptian mummies were ground up and sold as medicine. But that was just because it was the Middle Ages, right? Actually, "Merc Pharmaceuticals [not related to Merck] were making mummies into medicine up to 1924," said James Delay, vice president of exhibits for American Exhibitions. (*Morning Call*, June 19, 2011.)

"THE BEST SLINGERS [USERS OF THE SLING] CAME FROM THE BALEARIC ISLANDS, WHERE MOTHERS WOULD NOT ALLOW THEIR YOUNG SONS ANYTHING TO EAT UNLESS THEY WERE ABLE TO HIT THE DISH CONTAINING THEIR FOOD WITH A SLINGSHOT." (VEGETIUS, *MILITARY AFFAIRS* 1.16.) THE ISLAND'S NAME WAS ASSOCIATED WITH THE GREEK WORD *BALLEIN,* "TO THROW." (DIODORUS SICULUS, *LIBRARY OF HISTORY* 5.17.)

TRULY TRUNCATED

According to legend, famous Greek wrestler Milo of Croton died in the sixth century B.C., when he saw a tree trunk split with wedges and decided to test his strength by trying to divide the trunk with his bare hands. As he was exerting superhuman strength, the wedges fell to the ground and the trunk snapped shut around his hands. Milo's hands were trapped, and he was therefore unable to fend off an attacking gang of wolves that devoured him.

ANCIENT EGYPTIAN WOMEN PINCHED
THE BRIDE ON HER WEDDING DAY.

SADDLED WITH A NAME

Towns and cities are sometimes named after important people but Alexander III of Macedon (356–323 B.C.), also known as Alexander the Great, loved his horse Bucephalus (bull-head) so much that he named a city after him in his honor. According to Plutarch's *Life of Alexander* (6) and Arrian's *Anabasis Alexandri* (5.19), Bucephalus died after the Battle of the Hydaspes in 326 B.C. Here is an account by Aulus Gellius:

◉ Alexander was said to have paid seventy-eight thousand denarii for his horse Bucephalus, who, when equipped for battle, would allow no other rider. Once, grievously wounded and dying from a loss of blood, the animal safely removed Alexander from the battle and then fell down dead. In his honor, a city was built and named Bucephalon. (Aulus Gellius, *Attic Nights* 5.3.)

◉ The small town in Pakistan, which still exists, is called Phalia (Bucephalon). Since it's named after a horse I hope it is a very stable place.

STIRRUP SOME TROUBLE

Roman emperor Caligula (reigned A.D. 37 to 41) was known for a lot of cruelty but not so much for horsing around. Caligula had an unbridled affection for his white stallion, Incitatus (from the Latin adjective meaning "swift" or "at full gallop").

According to Suetonius's *Lives of the Twelve Caesars* (A.D. 121), Incitatus had "a marble stable, an ivory manger, purple housings, and a jeweled frontlet; he appointed a house, with a retinue of slaves, and fine furniture, for the reception of such as were invited in the horse's name to sup with him. It is even said that he intended to make him consul." (55.)

And Cassius Dio wrote, "Caligula used to invite Incitatus to dinner, where he would offer him golden barley and drink his health in wine from golden goblets; he swore by the life and fortune of Incitatus and even promised to appoint him consul, a promise that he would certainly have carried out if he had lived longer." (Cassius Dio, *Historia Romana* 69.)

Both of these quotes mention the fact that Caligula wanted to make his horse consul (the highest elected office of the Roman Republic). Some conclude that this was proof of Caligula's madness; others say it was an elaborate prank to basically rein in the Senate's power.

From Pi to Black Eye

Pythagoras of Samos (570–495 B.C.) was a Greek philosopher, mathematician, and founder of the religious movement called Pythagoreanism. He's also the guy who created the Pythagorean theorem ($a^2 + b^2 = c^2$). But he was far from being just a math nerd; he also had another famous equation: My Fist + Your Face = KO. Here's what Diogenes Laërtius had to say about the pugilistic mathematician:

> (Pythagoras), of whom we are speaking, was the first man who ever practiced boxing in a scientific manner, in the forty-eighth Olympiad, having his hair long, and being clothed in a purple robe; and that he was rejected from the competition among boys, and being ridiculed for his application, he immediately entered among the men, and came off victorious. (Laërtius, *Life of Pythagoras* 25.)

LIII

DISBELIEVERS

Watch out Miss Cleo, Sylvia Browne, John Edward, and the like. Cicero has been on to you guys for more than 2,100 years:

> Every day there is proof that astrology is useless. How many predictions do I remember Pompey, Crassus, and Caesar himself receiving from the astrologer that none of them would die other than in old age, at home and covered in glory? I am amazed that anyone could continue to put their trust in such people, when the falseness of their predictions is every day made clear by what actually happens. (Cicero, *On Divination* 2.99.)

"ASTROLOGERS HAVE VARIOUS ARGUMENTS THEY USE TO ESCAPE RESPONSIBILITY FOR THEIR PREDICTIONS. FOR EXAMPLE, THEY CLAIM THAT SPIRITS DO NOT OBEY, AND CANNOT BE SEEN BY, PEOPLE WITH FRECKLES." (PLINY, *NATURAL HISTORY* 30.16.)

SCRAWLED ON THE WALL

Here is the charming story of Successus, Severus, and Iris as played out on the walls of a bar in Pompeii (*Corpus Inscriptionum Latinarum* 4.8258, 4.8259):

- ☉ [Severus]: "Successus, a weaver, loves the innkeeper's slave girl named Iris. She, however, does not love him. Still, he begs her to have pity on him. His rival wrote this. Good-bye."

- ☉ [Answer by Successus]: "Envious one, why do you get in the way. Submit to a handsomer man and one who is being treated very wrongly and good looking."

- ☉ [Answer by Severus]: "I have spoken. I have written all there is to say. You love Iris, but she does not love you."

DON'T BE SO CYNICAL

Diogenes the Cynic (412–323 B.C.) was a Greek philosopher and one of the founders of Cynic philosophy. Unlike today's cynics, Cynics in ancient times didn't have a jaded distrust of everyone; their philosophy rejected all conventional desires for wealth, power, health, and fame, and called for living a simple life free from all possessions (what we would call hobos today). Diogenes took being a Cynic to its logical extreme, begging for a living and making his home out of a tub (perhaps a barrel or a large storage jar), in the marketplace. He was known for walking around in the daylight holding a lighted lantern. When asked about his actions, he would answer, "I am just looking for an honest man." Diogenes stated, however, that he only found rascals and scoundrels. (Diogenes Laërtius, *Lives and Opinions of Eminent Philosophers*, 2.6.32, 2.6.41)

Good thing Diogenes the Cynic never brought his lantern to Washington, D.C.

PLUCKING PLATO

One day Diogenes the Cynic (412–323 B.C.) heard Plato praising Socrates' definition of man as "a two-footed, featherless animal." According to Laërtius, "Diogenes plucked a cock and brought it into [Plato's] school, and said, 'This is Plato's man.' After this incident, the defination of man was amended with the words, 'with broad flat nails.'" (Diogenes Laërtius (3rd century A.D.), *Lives and Opinions of Eminent Philosophers*, Volume 2, VI:40)

LVII

SEEN ON AN ANCIENT
TOMBSTONE: HIC IACET
CORPUVS PVERI NOMINANDI
("HERE LIES THE BODY OF A
CHILD WHOSE NAME IS TO
BE ADDED.") APPARENTLY,
THE STONEMASON
ABSENTMINDEDLY COPIED THE
PROCEDURE FOR INSCRIPTIONS
INSTEAD OF ADDING THE
DEAD CHILD'S ACTUAL NAME.
(*L'ANNÉE ÉPIGRAPHIQUE* 112.)

ALEXANDER AND THE TERRIBLE, HORRIBLE, NO GOOD, VERY BAD DAY

People didn't usually mess with Alexander the Great, and if they did, they didn't live long enough to tell about it. But Diogenes the Cynic wasn't impressed or afraid of Alexander the Great. In fact, according to several sources, the two men met in Corinth, when Alexander sought out the Cynic. Alexander was excited to meet the eminent philosopher and found him sunning himself next to the barrel in which he lived. Alexander, who possessed great wealth and power, stood in front of the philosopher and said, "Ask any favor you choose of me." Diogenes replied, "Cease to shade me from the sun." (Cicero, *Tusculanae Quaestiones* 5.32; Plutarch, *Alexander* 14, *On Exile* 15; Diogenes Laërtius, *Lives and Opinions of Eminent Philosophers* 2.6.40.)

WHEN ALEXANDER NOTICED THE PHILOSOPHER LOOKING ATTENTIVELY AT A PILE OF HUMAN BONES, DIOGENES EXPLAINED, "I AM SEARCHING FOR THE BONES OF YOUR FATHER BUT CANNOT DISTINGUISH THEM FROM THOSE OF A SLAVE."

DEATH WISH

When asked how he wished to be buried, Diogenes the Cynic said he had left instructions to be thrown outside the city wall so wild animals could feast on his body. When asked if he minded this, he said, "Not at all, as long as you provide me with a stick to chase the creatures away!" When asked how he would use the stick since he would lack awareness, he replied, "If I lack awareness, then why should I care what happens to me when I am dead?" (Cicero, *Tusculanae Quaestiones* 1.42.)

LIVY (59 B.C.–A.D. 17) REPORTED THAT ABOUT 170 WOMEN FROM PRESTIGIOUS ROMAN FAMILIES WERE CONVICTED OF POISONING THEIR HUSBANDS IN 331 B.C. (*HISTORY OF ROME* 8.18.) OTHER CONTEMPORARY SOURCES GIVE EVEN LARGER NUMBERS.

HOT STUFF

The word "naphtha" comes from Latin and Greek and referred to any sort of flammable petroleum, pitch, or bitumen. Its various uses have had a long history. "Greek fire" was a sticky flammable mixture that was projected onto opponent's boats, and the Greek historian Thucydides mentions the use of tubed flamethrowers in the siege of Delium in 424 B.C. So why all the information? To let you know how crazy Alexander the Great was. As the Greek historian Strabo (63 B.C.–A.D. 24) recounts:

◎ The liquid kind, which they call naphtha, is of a singular nature; for if the naphtha is brought near fire it catches the fire; and if you smear a body with it and bring it near to the fire, the body bursts into flames; and it is impossible to quench these flames with water (for they burn more violently), unless a great amount is used, though they can be smothered and quenched with mud, vinegar, alum, and bird-lime. It is said that Alexander, for an experiment, poured some naphtha on a boy in a bath and brought a lamp near him; and that the boy, enveloped in flames, would have been nearly burned to death if the bystanders had not, by pouring on him a very great quantity of water, prevailed over the fire and saved his life. (Strabo, *Geography* 16.)

◎ In the second book of the Maccabees in the Septuagint—part of the Old Testament canon in some Christian denominations—the word "naphtha" refers to a miraculous flammable liquid.

What Would Uncle Remus Say?

According to Roman mythology, Romulus, who along with his brother Remus founded Rome, ensured that his city grew in population by demanding that the inhabitants rear all their male children and their firstborn daughters. Sounds all well and good. Romulus wanted children to be well taken care of . . . but not all children, apparently. He "forbade [parents] to destroy any children under three years of age unless they were maimed or monstrous from their very birth. These he did not forbid their parents to expose [leave outside to die of exposure], provided they first showed them to their five nearest neighbors and these also approved. Against those who disobeyed this law he fixed various penalties, including the confiscation of half their property." (Dionysius of Halicarnassus, *Roman Antiquities* 2.15.1–2.)

THE SLANG TERM USED BY ROMAN SOLDIERS FOR A MILITARY CAMP PITCHED ON DISADVANTAGEOUS AND UNEVEN GROUND WAS *NOVERCA*, "STEPMOTHER."

NURSES ORDERS

While poor Greek and Romans had to raise their own children, the children of the wealthy were routinely given over to the services of a wet nurse. In the second book of his four-volume treatise *Gynecology*, written in the second century A.D., Greek physician Soranus of Ephesus makes the following recommendations:

- A "wet nurse should be 'self controlled' so as to abstain from co-itus, drinking, lewdness . . . for coitus cools the affection toward the nursing by the diversion of sexual pleasure and moreover spoils and diminishes the milk."

- She should be even tempered and not superstitious, because "angry women are like maniacs and sometimes when the newborn cries from fear and they are unable to restrain it, they let it drop from their hands or overturn it dangerously."

- She should not drink, because she could be "harmed in soul as well as in body." He warns that the wet nurse could also "leave the baby untended or even fall down upon it in a dangerous way."

- Also, "the wet nurse should be tidy-minded lest the odor of the swaddling clothes cause the child's stomach to become weak and it lie awake on account of itching."

- Finally, "she should be Greek so that the infant nursed by her may become accustomed to the best speech." (*Gynecology* 19.88.)

A WOMAN SCORNED

Fulvia Flacca Bambula (83–40 B.C.) was reported to have stabbed Cicero's tongue after he was dead with her golden hairpins in retaliation for what he had uttered against Mark Antony. According to Cassius Dio, "Fulvia took the head into her hands before it was removed, and after abusing it spitefully and spitting upon it, set it on her knees, opened the mouth, and pulled out the tongue, which she pierced with the pins that she used for her hair, at the same time uttering many brutal jests." (*Roman History* 47.8.4.) Fulvia was a strong character, described by Velleius Paterculus as "a woman in body alone." (*Histories* 2.74.)

POMPONIA, THE WIDOW OF CICERO'S YOUNGER BROTHER QUINTUS TULLIUS, WHO WAS EXECUTED ALONG WITH HIS SON AND CICERO ON DECEMBER 7, 43 B.C., WAS OBVIOUSLY DISTRAUGHT. WHEN MARK ANTONY SENT HER PHILOLOGUS, THE FORMER SLAVE WHO HAD BETRAYED CICERO, SHE FORCED HIM TO CUT STRIPS OFF HIS OWN BODY, ROAST THEM, AND THEN EAT THEM. (PLUTARCH, *LIFE OF CICERO* 49.)

STUPID
ANCIENT
HISTORY

DIDN'T TRUST HIM TO DO IT RIGHT

"A woman urged her husband to commit suicide when she found that he had been suffering for a long time from putrescent ulcers of the groin, beyond hope of a cure. To make it easier for him, she tied herself to him and jumped out of a window into a lake." (Pliny, *Letters* 6.24.)

THE *LEX JULIA* (ROUGHLY, JULIAN LAWS) OF 18 B.C. DECREED THAT A FATHER COULD KILL HIS DAUGHTER IF SHE WERE CAUGHT IN THE ACT OF ADULTERY, PROVIDED THAT HER LOVER WAS ALSO KILLED. THE WOMAN'S HUSBAND HAD NO SUCH RIGHT BECAUSE HE WASN'T RELATED BY BLOOD. THERE WAS NO PENALTY, OR EVEN A LAW, CONCERNING THE ADULTEROUS BEHAVIOR OF HUSBANDS.

CERTAINLY NOT PISS POOR

Why does a lead pipe from the urinal in the Baths of Mithras at Ostia lead directly to a laundry? Ancient Roman secret. They used human and animal urine to keep their togas white and rarely let urine simply go down the drain. Laundries (or fulleries) even had collection vats for urine placed in front of their stores that men could use. (Some required a small price for the convenience.) The fuller would mix the urine with potash, carbonate of soda, and fuller's earth (a naturally occurring claylike substance) to form a detergent that was used to wash out all those pesky wine stains. Of course, it was the ammonia in the urine that did the trick. (Pliny, *Natural History* 28.18.26.)

LXIX

"URINE IS ALSO USED FOR TAKING OUT INK SPOTS. MALE URINE CURES GOUT; WITNESS THE FULLERS FOR INSTANCE, WHO, FOR THIS REASON, IT IS SAID, ARE NEVER TROUBLED WITH THAT DISEASE." (PLINY, *NATURAL HISTORY* 28.18.)

LEAVE WELL ENOUGH ALONE

Elagabalus (Marcus Aurelius Antoninus Augustus), also known as Heliogabalus, was Roman emperor from A.D. 218 to 222. During his four-year reign he certainly pissed a lot of people off. First, he married the vestal virgin Julia Aquilia Severa, which he wasn't supposed to do. Vestal virgins were highly honored priestesses who committed themselves before puberty and were sworn to celibacy for a period of thirty years. Then Elagabalus divorced her—which you weren't supposed to do, either. Then he married her again—which, of course, you weren't supposed to do. He was so hated by his countrymen that he was eventually assassinated. He was only eighteen years old at the time. (Cassius Dio, *Roman History* 79.9.)

"SOMETIMES WE CAN REFUTE A STATEMENT BY PRETENDING TO AGREE WITH IT. WHEN FABIA, DOLABELLA'S WIFE, CLAIMED TO BE THIRTY, CICERO SAID, 'THAT'S TRUE, FOR I'VE HEARD HER SAY IT FOR THE LAST TWENTY YEARS.'" (QUINTILIAN, *EDUCATION OF AN ORATOR* 6.3.73.)

TWO SIDES OF A SESTERCE

Although Emperor Elagabalus (A.D. 203–222) married and divorced five women, we know the names of only three of them. (Cassius Dio, *Roman History* 80.9.) His first wife was Julia Cornelia Paula, the second was the vestal virgin Julia Aquilia Severa, and then there was Annia Aurelia Faustina. (Herodian, *Roman History* 5.6.) Faustina was the widow of a man Elagabalus had had executed. But he soon divorced Faustina and remarried Severa. Sounds like a real ladies' man, right? Well, there's a question about that. According to Cassius Dio, his most unwavering relationship seems to have been with a blond slave from Caria named Hierocles, who was his chariot driver, but whom Elagabalus referred to as his husband. (Cassius Dio, *Roman History* 80.15.) Another account claims that Elagabalus actually married an athlete from Smyrna named Zoticus in a public ceremony at Rome. (*Historia augusta*, "Life of Elagabalus" 10.)

IN *ROMAN HISTORY*, CASSIUS
DIO WROTE THAT ELAGABALUS
WOULD PAINT HIS EYES,
SHAVE HIS HEAD, WEAR WIGS,
AND PROSTITUTE HIMSELF IN
TAVERNS, BROTHELS, AND EVEN
THE IMPERIAL PALACE. (80.14.)

A CLASSIC PRANK

Emperor Elagabalus invented a prototype whoopee cushion:

> Some of his humbler friends he would seat on air-pillows instead
> of on cushions and let out the air while they were dining, so that
> often the diners were suddenly found under the table. Finally,
> he was the first to think of placing a semi-circular group on the
> ground instead of on couches, with the purpose of having the air-
> pillows loosened by slaves who stood at the feet of the guests and
> the air thus let out. (*Historia augusta*, "Life of Elagabalus" 2.2.3.)

CALIGULA MADE ALL THREE
OF HIS SISTERS, AGRIPPINA THE
YOUNGER, JULIA DRUSILLA,
AND JULIA LIVILLA, HONORARY
VESTAL VIRGINS, EVEN THOUGH
THEY WERE ALL MARRIED.

WHAT'S IN A NAME?

A male Roman citizen typically had three names, a praenomen (a personal name), a nomen (a family name), and a cognomen (a particular branch of the family, or a nickname). In classic Roman fashion, known for excess, there was no limit to the number of cognomens an individual might affix to his name, but no one else comes close to this guy. Take a deep breath and let me introduce you to Quintus Pompeius Senecio Roscius Murena Coelius Sextus Julius Frontinus Silius Decianus Gaius Julius Eurycles Herculanus Lucius Vibullius Pius Augustanus Alpinus Bellicius Sollers Julius Aper Ducenius Produlus Rutilianus Rufinus Silius Valens Valerius Niger Claudius Fuscus Saxa Amyntianus Sosius Priscus, Roman consul in A.D. 169. His amazing thirty-six cognomens were found in a commemorative inscription at Tivoli, an ancient Italian town in Lazio, about eighteen miles east of Rome. (*Corpus Inscriptionum Latinarum* 14.3609.) He was obviously fond of the name Julius—he used it three times.

WHAT DID YOU CALL ME?

Most of us have heard the word "plebe" before, and when we have it was usually used in a derogatory way. But "plebs" was the name given to the group of free landowning Roman citizens, as distinguished from slaves and the *capite censi*, or "the head count," used to refer to the lowest class of citizens in ancient Rome. Members of the plebs were also distinct from the Roman aristocracy. In essence, the plebs were the middle class. In Roman days a plebeian could become quite wealthy and influential and even elevate his status. The emperor Nero, in fact, was born a plebian. He wasn't alone, either. Thirty percent of Roman emperors were plebs.

BABIES IN ANCIENT ROME WOULD
OFTEN BE REJECTED BY THEIR
PARENTS IF THEY WERE ILLEGITIMATE,
UNHEALTHY, DEFORMED, THE WRONG
SEX (FEMALE, FOR EXAMPLE), OR TOO
GREAT A BURDEN ON THE FAMILY.
LEAVING AN INFANT TO DIE TOOK
THE GUILT OFF THE PARENTS' HEADS
BECAUSE TECHNICALLY THEY DIDN'T
MURDER IT AS IT DIED NATURALLY
OF EXPOSURE TO THE ELEMENTS. THE
NAMES "PROIECTUS" AND "PROIECTICUS"
TRANSLATE TO, "THROWN OUT," AND
"STERCORIUS" SPECIFICALLY MEANS,
"LEFT ON A DUNG HEAP." ONE MILITARY
ADMINISTRATOR IN THE DANUBE
REGION IN A.D. 369 WHO OBVIOUSLY
WENT FROM DUNG HEAP TO THE TOP
OF THE HEAP WAS FLAVIUS STERCORIUS..
(*SELECT LATIN INSCRIPTIONS* 770.)

MESSAGES
FROM THE PAST IV

Graffiti from Pompeii, collected and recorded in the *Corpus Inscriptionum Latinarum*. The number after the location in parentheses is the catalog number of the inscription (not the date) in volume 4:

- ◎ (Atrium of a house of a large brothel) 1520: "Blondie has taught me to hate dark-haired girls. I shall hate them, if I can, but I wouldn't mind loving them. Pompeian Venus Fisica wrote this."

- ◎ (House of Caesius Valens and Herennius Nardus) 4637: "Rufus loves Cornelia Hele."

- ◎ (Atrium of the House of Pinarius) 6842: "If anyone does not believe in Venus, they should gaze at my girl friend."

- ◎ (House of the Tetrastyle Atrium) 2060: "Romula hung out here with Staphylus."

- ◎ (Vicolo del Panettiere, House of the Vibii, Merchants) 3117: "Atimetus got me pregnant."

- ◎ (Vicolo del Panettiere, House of the Vibii, Merchants) 3131: "Figulus loves Idaia."

- ◎ (House of Caprasius Primus) 3061: "I don't want to sell my husband, not for all the gold in the world."

- ◎ (Eumachia Building, Via della Abbondanza) 2048: "Secundus likes to screw boys."

CAESAR'S WIFE
MUST BE ABOVE SUSPICION

Julius Caesar, dictator of the Roman Republic (later the Roman Empire), was one of the most influential and powerful men in world history. He was a great military strategist and political leader who expanded the territory of the Roman Republic all the way to the Atlantic Ocean. With all these credentials it's a wonder why Caesar's nickname was "the Queen of Bithynia." In 80 B.C., young Julius Caesar was an ambassador to King Nicomedes IV in Bithynia, a Roman province in Asia Minor, and reportedly had a fling with the king. Most of the writers of the time mention the alleged affair, and Mark Antony even charged that Caesar's adopted son, Octavianus (Gaius Octavius after his adoption; he became Emperor Augustus Caesar), earned his adoption through sexual favors. Was Caesar really in love with Cleopatra or was he just in denial?

PEPI II NEFERKARE BECAME PHARAOH AT AGE SIX DURING THE SIXTH DYNASTY OF EGYPT'S OLD KINGDOM (2284–2184 B.C.). IN ORDER TO KEEP FLIES FROM LANDING ON HIM, PEPI II ALWAYS KEPT SEVERAL NAKED SLAVES NEARBY WHOSE BODIES WERE COVERED WITH HONEY.

SECRET DECODER RING

The state's political name in ancient Rome was "Roma." There was another name, too—a highly secret name used only in ancient rites called the Dionysian Mysteries. What was the secret word? It was "Amor," which is a palindromic word for "Roma" and also means "love." In the Roman Republic, a tribune was a title shared by elected officials who had the power to convene the Plebeian Council and to act as its president to propose legislation. A tribune named Valerius Soranus divulged the secret alternative name and was promptly executed, probably by crucifixion, which, although usually reserved for slaves and noncitizens, was sometimes used to also embarrass the family of the executed. (Servius on Virgil's *Aeneid* 1.277; Johannes Lydus, *On the Months* 4.73.)

DURING THE THIRD MACEDONIAN WAR (171–168 B.C.), KING PERSEUS WAS AFRAID THAT HIS HORSES WOULD BE FRIGHTENED BY THE WAR ELEPHANTS OF THE ROMAN ARMY. SO TO GET THEM USED TO IT HE HAD DUMMY ELEPHANTS CREATED, SMEARED WITH A NOXIOUS SMELLING PASTE, AND MADE TO EMIT "NOISES AS LOUD AS THUNDER." (CASSIUS DIO, *ROMAN HISTORY* 20.)

THE NAME GAME

Gaius Julius Caesar Augustus Germanicus (A.D. 12–41), also known as Gaius but more recognizable as Caligula, was Roman emperor from A.D. 37 to 41. Gaius's father, Germanicus, a much beloved public figure, was the nephew and adopted son of Emperor Tiberius and a greatly admired Roman general. Gaius came from a powerful bloodline, so how did he wind up with the name "Caligula"? Well, Caligula was a nickname that he got as a small boy from soldiers while he accompanied his father on military campaigns. It means "little soldier's boot," or "little army boot." He never referred to himself as Caligula. Seneca explains that the grown Gaius didn't like his nickname at all:

> A front-rank centurion angered the emperor Gaius by calling him Caligula. Since he was born in camp and had been brought up among soldiers, this is what he used to be called, and he was never so well known to the soldiers by any other name, but once he started to wear big boots he considered Caligula an insult and a disgrace. (*On Firmness* 18.)

WHAT EVER HAPPENED TO JUST PLAIN FIDO?

Lucius Junius Moderatus Columella (A.D. 4–70) is considered by scholars to be the most important writer on agriculture of the Roman Empire. He covered a lot of ground in his twelve-volume book *De re rustica* (*On Agriculture*)—even what to call your dog. He wrote: "So that each dog may hear quickly and accurately when it is called, they should not be given long names, nor names shorter than two syllables. For example, Greek names such as Skylax ["Puppy"] and Lakon ["Spartan"], Latin ones such as Ferox ["Fierce"] and Celer ["Swift"]; for bitches, Greek names such as Spoudé ["Haste"], Alké ["Vigor"], Romé ["Strength"], Latin names such as Lupa ["She-wolf"], Cerva ["Deer"], Tigis ["Tigress"]. (Columella *De re rustica* 7.12.13.) Columella was probably influenced by Xenophon of Athens (430–354 B.C.), who created a list of forty-seven names for dogs in his book *Cynegeticus* (*Hunting with Dogs*). Every canine's name is two syllables.

ACTS TO DIE FOR II

The Bible and the Torah are filled with crimes worthy of death.
Here are a few more you should be aware of and avoid:

- Psychics, wizards, and so on are to be stoned to
  death. (Leviticus 20:27.)

- If a priest's daughter is a whore, she is to be burnt at the
  stake. (Leviticus 21:9.)

- "He that smiteth his father, or his mother, shall be surely
  put to death." (Exodus 21:15 KJV.)

- "He that sacrificeth unto any god, save unto the LORD
  only, he shall be utterly destroyed." (Exodus 22:20 KJV.)

- "Thou shalt not suffer a witch to live." (Exodus 22:18 KJV.)

- "But if the ox . . . hath killed a man or a woman; the ox
  shall be stoned, and his owner also shall be put to death."
  (Exodus 21:29 KJV.)

- "If a man have a stubborn and rebellious son, which
  will not obey the voice of his father, or the voice of his
  mother . . . all the men of his city shall stone him with
  stones, that he die." (Deuteronomy 21:18–21 KJV.)

THERE ARE NO ACCIDENTS

How did Rome become the cultural center of the universe in ancient times? It happened when Crates of Mallus (who is also famous for constructing the earliest known globe of the Earth) came to Rome as an ambassador from the king (either Eumenes II, in 168 B.C., or Attalus II in 159 B.C.) of Pergamum (in modern western Turkey). According to Suetonius, in his book *De grammaticis*, before Crates there was no study of grammar or criticism among the Romans. So did this great thinking man know that it was his destiny to come to Rome and bring enlightenment? No, actually Crates accidentally fell into the Cloaca Maxima (main drain) near the Palatine Hill and broke his leg. He had to stay in Rome for several months while his leg healed. He needed money so he opened a school.

THE LATIN WORD FOR A
MILITARY CAMP, *CASTRA*,
WAS DERIVED IN COMMON
LANGUAGE FROM THE ADJECTIVE
CASTUS, MEANING "CHASTE,"
OR FROM THE VERB *CASTRARE*,
MEANING "CASTRATE," SINCE
THE SOLDIERS HAD TO REMAIN
"CHASTE" WHILE ON DUTY, AND
BEING IN CAMPS MEANT THEIR
SEXUAL DESIRE WAS CASTRATED.
THE ROMAN EMPEROR LUCIUS
SEPTIMIUS SEVERUS (RULED
A.D. 193–211) WAS THE FIRST TO
PERMIT SOLDIERS SERVING IN
THE MILITARY TO MARRY.

REAL TROOPERS

We all know that the Romans prided themselves on being organized. They were so organized, in fact, that they even planned what time of the year they would go to war. You see, the Romans were very much an agricultural people, so they couldn't afford to fight wars during planting season or at harvest, and winter was too cold and snowy to move troops, so the Roman military engaged in attacks only during the summer. Roman historian Titus Livius (59 B.C.–A.D. 17), known as Livy, wrote about the debate concerning continuing the siege of the Etruscan city of Veli (around 396 B.C.) during the winter months:

> If a war is not finished in the summer, our soldiers must learn to wait through the winter and not, like summer birds, look around for shelter as soon as autumn comes. The pleasure of hunting carries men off through snow and frost to the mountains and the woods: Should we not apply to the demands of war the same endurance as is elicited by sport and pleasure? (Livy, *History of Rome* 5.6.)

DOGS OF WAR

In A.D. 272, Lucius Domitius Aurelianus (A.D. 215–275), also known as Aurelian, was a Roman emperor who was entangled in a frustrating war of resistance after he besieged Tyana (in modern south-central Turkey). The *Historia augusta* tells the tale of how a hardened Roman emperor had a change of heart: "In his frustration at the prolonged siege, he declared, 'I shall not leave a dog in this town.' By the time Tyana fell, Aurelian had decided to be merciful to the citizens and told his soldiers to kill only the dogs. Despite being deprived of their expected plunder, the troops took his decision in good spirit, as if it were a joke." (*Historia augusta*, "Life of Aurelian" 22.)

XC

IN A.D. 60, WHEN NERO'S GREAT GENERAL GNAEUS DOMITIUS CORBULO (BROTHER-IN-LAW OF THE EMPEROR CALIGULA) WAS BESIEGING THE ARMENIAN CAPITAL OF TIGRANOCERTA, HE CAME UP WITH A BRILLIANT STRATEGY TO FORCE THEIR SURRENDER. HE CATAPULTED THE HEAD OF A CAPTURED ARMENIAN NOBLEMAN OVER THEIR DEFENSIVE WALL. IT LANDED RIGHT IN THE MIDDLE OF A COUNCIL MEETING. THE ARMENIANS SURRENDERED. (FRONTINUS, *STRATAGEMS* 2.9.)

TO THE VICTOR GOES THE SPOILS

One of the perks of being the victor in a war is that the winner always gets to write the history. Therefore, records of battle casualties are rarely reliable. The Romans killed twenty-five thousand Samnites and Gauls during the Battle of Sentinum (295 B.C.), according to Livy. (*History of Rome* 10.29.) But another historian, Diodorus Siculus, calculated the enemy loss at one hundred thousand. (*The Library* 21.4.) In the 60s B.C., a law was passed to try to keep generals honest about battle death tolls. (Valerius Maximus, *Memorable Deeds and Sayings* 2.8.1.) The law was intended to curtail such outrageous claims as given by Roman generals after the Battle of Artaxata in 68 B.C. According to Plutarch, the Armenians lost a hundred thousand of their infantry and cavalry, while the Romans suffered only a hundred wounded and five dead. (*Life of Lucullus* 28.)

THE GREEK HISTORIAN STRABO (63 B.C.–A.D. 24) REPORTED THAT DURING AN EXPEDITION TO ARABIA, TEN THOUSAND OF THE ENEMY WERE SLAUGHTERED WHEREAS THE ROMANS LOST ONLY TWO MEN. (*GEOGRAPHY* 16.4.24.)

ALL'S FAIR IN LOVE AND WAR

When Spartacus (109–71 B.C.) and his army were trapped by the Romans during the Third Servile War (73–71 B.C.) he outfoxed the Romans by leading them to believe he had a much larger army than he actually did. Spartacus tied soldiers who had died in battle on stakes outside his camp and equipped them with weapons, helmets, and armor. This gave the illusion, especially at a distance, that Spartacus had hundreds of sentries guarding the camp. (Frontinus, *Stratagems* 1.5.22.)

IT TAKES A LOT

When a Roman military unit, or legion, was found guilty of dereliction of duty or—worse—mutiny, one course of punishment that could befall them was *deimatio*. Although "decimate" is derived from the word, *deimatio* didn't mean wholesale destruction. The punishment of *deimatio* was that every tenth (*decimus*) man in the unit would be beaten, whipped, or stoned to death. The punishment was based on the drawing of lots, so individual innocence or guilt didn't matter—it was basically up to the gods to decide who got punished. "When a defeated army is punished with decimation, brave men are also chosen by lot. Setting an example on a large scale always involves a degree of injustice, when individuals suffer to ensure the pubic good." (Tacitus, *Annals* 14.44.)

HE'S ONE IN A HUNDRED

Macrinus (Marcus Opellius Macrinus; A.D. 165–218), Roman emperor from 217 to 218, "was arrogant and bloodthirsty and desirous of ruling in military fashion. . . . For he even crucified soldiers and always used the punishments meted out to slaves, and when he had to deal with a mutiny among the troops, he usually decimated the soldiers—but sometimes he only centimated them [*centum* for one hundred—executing one person in one hundred]. This last was an expression of his own, for he used to say that he was merciful in putting to death only one in a hundred, whereas they deserved to have one in ten or one in twenty put to death." (*Historia augusta*, "Life of Opellius Macrinus" 12.1.2.3.)

XCVI

HANNIBAL RISING

Generally considered one of the greatest military commanders in history, Hannibal, son of Hamilcar Barca (247–182 B.C.), was a Carthaginian military commander and brilliant tactician. Here's an example of his skills as related by a Roman biographer, Cornelius Nepos (100–25 B.C.):

> When Hannibal was in exile from Carthage, he commanded the troops of King Prusias of Bithynia against King Eumenes of Pergamum. Outnumbered in a sea battle, he knew his only hope was to capture Eumenes himself. He identified Eumenes's ship by sending an emissary with a letter for him, ostensibly with peace terms (but actually making fun of him). He watched to see to which ship the emissary was directed and concentrated his attack on it, ordering his men to distract the crews of the other enemy ships by bombarding them with pottery jars full of poisonous snakes. (Cornelius Nepos, *Hannibal* 10.)

DON'T TAKE THINGS SO LITERALLY

According to Valerius Maximus's book *Memorable Deeds and Sayings* (7.3.4), after the Romans' victory over Seleucid king Antiochus III the Great in 188 B.C., a peace treaty was signed that gave the Romans half of the king's ship as spoils of war. Quintus Fabius Labeo, in a cunningly linguistic turnabout, ordered all of Antiochus's boats cut in half.

MAN IS A POLITICAL ANIMAL

After Mount Vesuvius erupted in A.D. 79 and completely covered the cities of Pompeii and Herculaneum they were never rebuilt—they stood frozen in time until their accidental rediscovery in 1749. Archaeologists were amazed to uncover exactly how people lived in ancient times and how some things haven't changed after centuries of evolution—such as politics. There were almost three thousand municipal election notices on walls in Pompeii. Several supported Marcus Cerrinius Vatia for city magistrate (*Select Latin Inscriptions* 6418a, b, c); others were not so supportive:

- "The petty thieves ask you to elect Vatia as city magistrate."

- "Macerio and those who sleep a lot ask you to elect Vatia as city magistrate."

- "All the late drinkers ask you to elect Marcus Cerrinius Vatia as city magistrate."

(*Corpus Inscriptionum Latinarum* 4.7621.)

GREAT CAESAR'S GHOST

Plutarch (Lucius Mestrius Plutarchus when he became a Roman citizen), in his book *Life of Julius Caesar*, penned a story that when Caesar was a young man, pirates captured him and demanded a twenty talents ransom for his release. Caesar, being Caesar, was aghast at the paltry amount of ransom and demanded they increase it to fifty talents. A talent is a unit of measurement, not a currency, so a talent of gold or silver was actually a substantial amount of money (in some cases one talent of silver represented nine man-years of skilled work). During the thirty-eight days Caesar was held captive, awaiting the payment of the ransom, he frequently threatened the pirates that he would come back for them and personally have them crucified. The pirates thought he was joking until Caesar made good on his threat. (Plutarch, *Life of Julius Caesar* 2.)

C

CURSE OF THE MUMMY

On February 17, 1923, a little more than three months after the discovery of King Tut's tomb, a crowd of about twenty invited guests crowded together to watch the unsealing of the burial chamber in Egypt's famous Valley of the Kings. This startling find not only was an archaeologist's dream, it also started a fashion craze with scarab-beetle jewelry, pharaoh blouses, and so forth, and created the legend of the mummy's curse. You see, a short two months after the tomb was opened, the project's financier, George Herbert, 5th Earl of Carnarvon, died of complications from a mosquito bite. Then his dog died. Then other people connected in a roundabout way to the dig began to die under suspicious circumstances.

So was there a real curse? Not really. Eighty years after the tomb's discovery, the *British Medical Journal* published a scientific study by Mark R. Nelson called "One Foot in the Past. The Mummy's Curse: Historical Cohort Study," in which the author examined the survival rates of those Westerners (no native Egyptians) that tomb founder Howard Carter identified as being in Egypt during the examination of the tomb. There were forty-four people in total but only twenty-five were actually present during an opening or examination; on average those twenty-five "exposed people" lived 20.8 years after the opening of the tomb, while the unexposed lived 28.9 years. (*British Medical Journal 32* [December 21–28, 2002]: pp. 1482–84.)

MAN HE'S OVERBOARD

G aius Plinius Secundus (A.D. 23– 79), better known as Pliny the Elder, was more than just an author, naturalist, and natural philosopher; he was also a naval and army commander of the early Roman Empire. Pliny was commander of the ancient port in Campania, in southern Italy, known at that time as Misenum (now Miseno in the Italian Province of Naples). He had some interesting thoughts on ships, seamen, and seafaring. For example:

- "Pouring vinegar over ships gives them some slight protection against cyclones." (*Natural History* 2.132.)

- "I have it on the authority of some distinguished members of the equestrian order that they saw a merman exactly like a human being in the sea near Cadiz. He climbs on board ships in the night time, they say, and part of the deck where he sits is immediately weighed down, and ships are actually sunk if he stays on board too long." (*Natural History* 9.10.)

STUPID
ANCIENT
HISTORY

THAT'S NOT A PIG IN THAT POKE

The Romans, of course, had lots of laws on the books, but Rome's earliest legal code, the Twelve Tables, established in the mid–fifth century B.C., was silent on the subject of murder. In ancient times, retribution for murder was left up to the decedent's family to mete out. But if that didn't work, here's how some murderers were dealt with:

The traditional punishment for parricide [killing a parent or another close relative] is as follows: the condemned person is beaten with blood-colored sticks, then sewn up in a sack with a dog, a rooster, a viper, and a monkey, and thrown into the deep sea, if the sea is nearby; otherwise, in accordance with the law passed by the deified Hadrian, he is thrown to wild beasts. (*Justinian's Digest* 48.9.9.)

IN 100 B.C., PUBLICIUS MALLEUS, WHO HAD BEEN FOUND GUILTY OF MURDERING HIS MOTHER, WAS THE FIRST TO BE SEWN IN A SACK AND THROWN INTO THE SEA. (LIVY, *HISTORY OF ROME* 68.)

THE MORE THINGS CHANGE, THE MORE THEY STAY THE SAME

An excerpt from Valerius Maximus, *Memorable Deeds and Sayings* (8.2.2.):

Gaius Visellius Varro was afflicted with a serious illness, and because he had had a sexual affair with Otacilia, the wife of Laterensis, he allowed her to record in his books that she had advanced him 300,000 sesterces. His plan was that if he died, she could demand that sum from his heirs. He wanted it to be a kind of legacy, but he disguised his generous payment for sexual pleasure by pretending it was a debt. But then, contrary to Otacilia's hopes, he escaped from that storm.

Otacilia was annoyed because Varro had not brought her hopes of gain to fruition by dying, so she suddenly changed from an obliging girlfriend and started acting openly as a profiteer and demanding the money. She had been trying to get at that money all along by using her own shameless impudence and Varro's worthless promise. Gaius Aquillius, a man of great prestige . . . dismissed her case, but would certainly have found both for and against Varro if the same legal formula had allowed it.

Other than the language it sounds like it came right out of a contemporary television drama—but this case took place around 66 B.C.

You Say Yes, I Say No

It may seem weird but the Latin language has no simple single word for "yes," nor is there a simple single word for "no." For "yes," phrases such as *ita vero* ("so indeed") or *sic* ("it is so") or *audio* (basically, "I hear you") are used. *Minime* ("Not in the least") and *non audio* ("I don't hear you") are used to express disagreement.

For a direct question, the Romans usually began with either *Nonne* or *num*, depending on the expected answer. *Nonne* expects a yes answer; *num* expects a no answer. So, in Roman times, there was no such thing as a yes or no answer.

MESSAGES
FROM THE PAST V

Graffiti from Pompeii, collected and recorded in the *Corpus Inscriptionum Latinarum*. The number after the location in parentheses is the catalog number of the inscription (not the date) in volume 4:

- (The Lupinare) 2175: "I screwed a lot of girls here."

- (The Lupinare) 2185: "On June 15th, Hermeros screwed here with Phileterus and Caphisus."

- (The Lupinare) 2192: "Sollemnes, you screw well!"

- (Vico d' Eumachia, small room of a possible brothel) 2146: "Vibius Restitutus slept here alone and missed his darling Urbana."

- (House of Verus, between the two doors of the house) 4838: "Secundus says hello to his friends."

- (Street of the theaters) 64: "A copper pot went missing from my shop. Anyone who returns it to me will be given 65 bronze coins [sestertii]. 20 more will be given for information leading to the capture of the thief."

- (Above a bench outside the Marine Gate) 1751: "If anyone sits here, let him read this first of all: if anyone wants a screw, he should look for Attice; she costs 4 *sestertii*."

STOP CRYING, IT'S THE LAW!

"Since the period of mourning starts immediately after a person dies, a woman who finds out about her husband's death after the statutory period of mourning has expired puts on her mourning dress and also takes it off again on the same day." (*Justinian's Digest* 3.2.8.) "Men are not under compulsion to mourn the death of their wives." (*Justinian's Digest* 3.2.9.)

CVII

LEGAL HISTORY

In ancient Rome, long before the advent of the Christian Bible, Romans would swear to "tell the truth, the whole truth, and nothing but the truth" by placing their right hand on their testicles. It is from this ritual that we derived the terms *testi*mony" and *testi*fy." I wonder what happened when a woman was called to the witness stand?

CVIII

SAINT SILVERIUS, WHO RULED THE VATICAN AS POPE FROM JUNE 8, 536, UNTIL MARCH 537 A.D., WAS THE SON OF POPE HORMISDAS, WHO LEFT OFFICE IN 523 A.D. THIS IS OFTEN REFERRED TO AS THE "MIRACLE OF THE GREAT COINCIDENCE."

BEARING FALSE WITNESS II

Here are a few more misquoted, misunderstood, and misused missives from the main man's manuscript:

"Money is the root of all evil." This is a great condemnation of people who pursue wealth, and it's also one of the all-time misquoted passages from the Bible. According to 1 Timothy 6:10, "The *love* of money is the root of all evil." Thus the Apostle Paul, who authored this chapter in the Bible, wasn't bad-mouthing money itself, but the people who focus on money to the detriment of everything and everybody else.

"The Lord works in mysterious ways." This phrase isn't anywhere in the Bible, and there's not really even a comparative verse. It actually comes from an old hymn written by William Cowper (1731–1800):

> God moves in a mysterious way
> His wonders to perform;
> He plants His footsteps in the sea
> And rides upon the storm.

DEATH ON THE CROSS

Most Western people know about crucifixion only because of the biblical story of Jesus's execution (Matthew 27:38; Mark 15:27–28; Luke 23:33; John 19:18). But crucifixion was one of the most popular forms of corporal punishment in the Roman era. Countless thousands of people were crucified in the Roman Empire. Roman citizens were exempt under all circumstances. (Cicero, *In verrem* 1.7, 3.2, 3.24, 3.26, 4.10.) The following crimes were worthy of crucifixion: piracy, highway robbery, assassination, forgery, false testimony, mutiny, high treason, rebellion. (Pauly-Wissowa, *Real-Encyclopedia*, s.v. "Crucifixion"; Josephus, *Bellum Judaicum* 5.11.1.)

Soldiers who aided and abetted the enemy and slaves who denounced their masters were also punished by death on the cross. There were several different styles of crosses—the "t" shaped, the "X" or Saint Andrews Cross, and the "T." The traditional way of crucifixion is that a stake (*palus*) was embedded firmly in the ground (*crucem figere*) before the condemned arrived at the place of execution. (Cicero, *In verrem* 5.12; Josephus, *Bellum Judaicum* 7.6.4.) The crossbeam (*patibulum*), bearing the *titulus*, the inscription naming the crime (Matthew 27:37; Luke 23:38; Suetonius, *Caligula* 38), and from which the condemned would be nailed, was carried to the site by the one being executed. (Plutarch, *De sera num. vind.* 9; Matthew 27:37; John 19:17.)

IT's GOOD TO BE THE KING

Ramses II (1303–1213 B.C.), also referred to as Ramses the Great, was the third Egyptian pharaoh (1279–1213 B.C.) of the Nineteenth Dynasty. In 1975, Egyptologists visiting his tomb discovered that the mummified remains of Ramses were in a state of deterioration and proposed that he be sent to France for a face-lift. The transfer was proposed by French president Valéry Giscard d'Estaing during his meeting with Egyptian president Anwar Sadat in Cairo in December 1975, but a mummy of Ramses's stature is wrapped in more than linen—it's also wrapped in red tape. Eventually everything was worked out and, believe it or not, Ramses II was issued an Egyptian passport that listed his occupation as "King (deceased)" so he could board a flight to France. He arrived in Le Bourget Airport on September 26, 1976, with the full military honors befitting a living king. (*New Scientist*, November 13, 2004; *Avalanche Journal*, September 27, 1976.)

THE ARCTIC AND ANTARCTIC
WERE NAMED BY THE GREEK
PHILOSOPHER ARISTOTLE
(384–322 B.C.). THE LANDMASS
TO THE NORTH "LAY UNDER
THE CONSTELLATION OF
ARKTOS, THE BEAR; SO MUST
THE SOUTHERN LANDS
BE UNDER THE OPPOSITE:
ANTARKTIKOS," HE WROTE.

JUST WHAT THE DOCTOR ORDERED

- ◎ "Touching the nostrils of a she-mule with one's lips is said to stop sneezing and hiccups." (Pliny, *Natural History* 28.57.)

- ◎ "If a person whispers in a donkey's ear that he has been stung by a scorpion, the affliction is immediately transferred to the donkey." (Pliny, *Natural History* 28.155.)

- ◎ "Sexual intercourse is good for lower back pain, for weakness of the eyes, for derangement, and for depression." (Pliny, *Natural History* 28.58.)

TAKE THIS AND
CALL ME IN THE MORNING

◎ "It is said that if someone takes a stone or some other missile that has slain three living creatures—a human being, a wild boar, and a bear—at three blows, and throws it over the roof of a house in which there is a pregnant woman, she will immediately give birth, however difficult her labor may be." (Pliny, *Natural History* 28.33.)

◎ "Strains and bruises are treated with wild boar's dung gathered in spring and dried. This treatment is used for those who have been dragged by a chariot or mangled by its wheels or bruised in any way. Fresh dung also may be smeared on." (Pliny, *Natural History* 28.237.)

CXV

TUT, TUT, TUT

King Tutankhamen is one of the most popular pharaohs because of all the riches found in his undisturbed tomb. How he died at such a young age has always been a mystery, though there are several theories. One of the most popular is that his right-hand man, Ay, the highest official to serve the king, killed him. When X-rays were conducted on King Tut's head, a crack was discovered that led people to believe that he was murdered. Ay, having the most to gain from his death—most notably the throne—was the chief suspect.

But in 2005, a CT scan of the Boy King revealed that he had a fracture on the left leg, which, according to leading Egyptologist Dr. Zahi Hawass, could have become infected and was the real cause of Tut's death. The crack in the skull, Hawass suggests, actually occurred after Tut died and was caused by careless mummy makers. DNA analysis conducted in 2010 showed the presence of malaria in King Tut's system. It is believed that these two conditions (malaria and a leg infection) led to his death. Not as sexy as a murder, but at least the mummy mystery has been unraveled.

THE DOCTOR WILL SEE YOU NOW

"A man's urine in which a lizard has been drowned is an anti-aphrodisiac [dulls sexual desire] potion; so also are snails and pigeon's droppings drunk with olive oil and wine. The right section of a vulture's lung worn as an amulet in a crane's skin is a powerful aphrodisiac, as is consuming the yolks of five dove eggs mixed with a denarius of pig fat and honey, or sparrows or sparrow's eggs, or wearing as an amulet a rooster's right testicle wrapped in ram's skin." (Pliny, *Natural History* 30.141.)

"IF ONE WISHES A CHILD TO BE BORN WITH BLACK EYES, THE MOTHER SHOULD EAT A SHREW DURING HER PREGNANCY." (PLINY, *NATURAL HISTORY* 30.134.)

STUPID
ANCIENT
HISTORY

LIE DOWN ON THE COUCH

Long before Sigmund Freud, Alfred Adler, Carl Jung, and others pioneered and practiced psychoanalysis, there was Artemidorus Daldianus (Daldis in southwest Turkey), also known as Ephesius, who lived in the second century and was a professional diviner. He is known for his five-volume work *Oneirocritica* (*The Interpretation of Dreams*). Here are some of his dream analyses:

- ◎ "Dreaming about turnips, rutabagas, and pumpkins presages disappointed hopes, since they are massive but lack nutritional value. They signify surgery and woundings with iron implements for sick people and travelers, respectively, since these vegetables are cut into slices." (*Oneirocritica* 1.67.)

- ◎ "Dreaming that one is dead or is being crucified foretells marriage for a bachelor." (*Oneirocritica* 2.49, 2.53.)

"FURTHERMORE, THE PENIS IS ALSO A [DREAM] SIGN OF WEALTH AND POSSESSIONS BECAUSE IT ALTERNATELY EXPANDS AND CONTRACTS AND BECAUSE IT IS ABLE TO PRODUCE AND TO ELIMINATE."

(*ONEIROCRITICA* 1.45.)

A SALTY STORY

I t's so common today it's even referred to as common: common table salt. Salt is in such abundance these days it only makes sense that it was always readily available—but it wasn't. In fact, salt was very expensive and not always easy to come by right up to the 1900s. Traders in ancient Greece bartered their slaves for salt, and a lazy or unruly slave was considered "Not worth his salt"—an insult still in use today. Our word "salary" dates back to Roman times when soldiers were paid an allowance, called, in Latin, a *salarium argentums* (which translates to "salt money"), so they could buy salt. The Latin words for "well-being" *salus*, and for "health," *salubritas*, both derive from the Latin *sal*, meaning "salt." In Mali, West Africa, salt was once worth its weight in gold; another way of looking at it was gold was worth its weight in salt.

IN 2200 B.C., UNDER ORDERS FROM CHINA'S EMPEROR YÜ, THE WORLD'S FIRST TAX WAS LEVIED ON SALT.

STUPID
ANCIENT
HISTORY

BETTER THAN SAYING YOU'RE SORRY

"If one regrets having inflicted a blow, whether struck at close quarters or with a missile, and then immediately spits into the palm of one's hand, the person who has been struck immediately feels less aggrieved. This may seem incredible, but it is easy to confirm it by putting it to the test." Pliny, *Natural History* 28.36.)

CXXI

THAT'S NOT A POEM— THAT'S A LONGFELLOW

According to an account in *Roman History* (52.29) by Cassius Dio (A.D. 150–235), the Emperor Nero decided it was up to him to write an epic poem on the history of Rome but questioned how long it should be. A number of Nero's yes men said the poem should be four hundred books in length (by contrast, Virgil's *Aeneid* has twelve books; Ovid's *Metamorphoses* has fifteen; and Silius Italicus's *Punica* has seventeen). When the Stoic philosopher Lucius Annaeus Cornutus, who wrote the *Compendium of Greek Theology*, told Nero that no one would read a four-hundred-book poem Nero banished him from the city. By the way, Nero never got around to writing the poem. Guess he was too busy fiddling about. (Cassius Dio, *Roman History* 62.29.)

THE EYE OF RA

Ancient Egyptians were known for their elaborate makeup, especially makeup that extenuated the eyes. But they didn't do this for purely cosmetic reasons. They believed that the makeup had healing powers, warded off illness, and evoked the protection of the Gods Horus and Ra. A study released on January 15, 2010, in *Analytical Chemistry*, a semimonthly journal of the American Chemical Society, shows that the makeup did, in fact, have a medicinal effect. The study found that the makeup primarily consisted of four lead-based chemicals: galena, which produced dark tones and gloss, and the white materials cerussite, laurionite, and phosgenite. In ancient Egypt, during periods when the Nile flooded, Egyptians were susceptible to severe eye infections that caused disease and inflammation. It turns out that the lead had antibacterial properties that helped prevent a lot of those infections. It looked pretty cool, too. (Isa Tapsoba, et al., "Finding Out Egyptian Gods' Secret Using Analytical Chemistry: Biomedical Properties of Egyptian Black Makeup Revealed by Amperometry at Single Cells," *Analytical Chemistry* 82, no. 2 [2010]: pp. 457–60.)

GIVE OR TAKE A
FEW THOUSAND MILES

The earth has a circumference of slightly more than 24,900 miles at the equator (24,901.55 miles, if you must know). In the third century B.C., Eratosthenes of Cyrene (276–195 B.C.), a Greek mathematician, poet, athlete, geographer, astronomer, and music theorist, calculated it as 24,700 miles. But for some reason people decided not to use Eratosthenes's nearly spot-on calculation and instead, for more than fifteen hundred years, relied on the miscalculation of 17,800 miles proposed by Claudius Ptolemy of Alexandria (A.D. 90–168). This erroneous calculation of the earth's circumference was partly responsible for Columbus's assumption that he could find a short route to India through the Caribbean.

ERATOSTHENES OF CYRENE WAS ALSO THE PERSON WHO COINED THE WORD "GEOGRAPHY"; INVENTED THE MODERN DISCIPLINE OF GEOGRAPHY; INVENTED A SYSTEM OF LATITUDE AND LONGITUDE; AND CALCULATED, WITH AMAZING ACCURACY, THE TILT OF THE EARTH'S AXIS. HE IS ALSO CREDITED WITH ACCURATELY CALCULATING THE DISTANCE FROM THE EARTH TO THE SUN AND INVENTING THE LEAP DAY.

RUB-A-DUB-DUB

"Soap was invented by the Gauls for reddening the hair. It is made from animal fat and ashes. The best type is made from beechwood ash and goat fat. It can be either solid or liquid. The Germans also use it, the men more than the women." (Pliny, *Natural History* 28.191.) The Greeks and Romans did not use soap for washing. Their preferred method was to slather on some scented olive oil and then scrape off the oil, dirt, and grease with a small curved metal tool called a strigil.

STRIGILS WERE USED IN ROMAN BATHS AND WERE MADE
IN DIFFERENT SIZES FOR DIFFERENT BODY PARTS.

IT TAKES ALL KINDS

Pliny the Elder's book *Natural History* is one of the most fascinating books ever written. There are some amazing stories included; some that seem a little too amazing. I'm sure parts of his book were like the *National Enquirer* of the day.

"In the Baltic Sea, there are islands inhabited by people whose ears are so enormous that they cover their bodies with them and do not need clothes." (Pliny, *Natural History* 4.95.)

"By contract, the Shade-Foot people of India keep themselves cool by lying on their backs and shading themselves from the sun with their single enormous foot." (Pliny, *Natural History* 7.23.)

"Also in India are found the Mouthless people, who live on air and the odor of roots, flowers, and apples; it is said that they may die if subjected to a particularly strong smell." (Pliny, *Natural History* 7.25.)

PLAY NICE WITH OTHERS

Claudius Aelianus (A.D. 175–235), often referred to as Aelian, was a Roman author and teacher of rhetoric. He spoke Greek so perfectly that he was called "honey-tongued" (*meliglossos*), but I bet some of the people he wrote about have other names for him. Here's what he had to say about the Byzantines:

> The people of Byzantium are said to be so amazingly addicted to wine that they live in taverns and rent their homes to people visiting the city. . . . When the enemy were attacking the walls during a determined siege, the Byzantines drifted away and spent the day in their usual haunts. So Leonides, their commander, had taverns set up for them on the walls. By this trick, he finally managed to persuade them not to desert their posts. (Aelian, *Varia historia* 3.14.)

STOP WINEING

Roman author Claudius Aelianus didn't suffer fools or drunkards, and he wasn't afraid to write about them, either.

"The Nation of the Tapyrians is so addicted to Wine, that they live in Wine, and bestow the greatest part of their life and conversation upon it. Neither do they abuse it by drinking only, but by anointing themselves therewith, as others do with Oil." (Aelian, *Varia historia* 3.13.)

"The Argives also and Corinthians have been reproached in Comedies for being intemperately addicted to Wine. Of the Thracians it is at this time reported for certain, that they are great Drinkers." (Aelian, *Varia historia* 3.15.)

"WHEN A LION IS SICK, NOTHING WILL CURE HIM BUT TO EAT AN APE." (AELIAN, *VARIA HISTORIA* 1.9.)

ALL ABOARD

" If a woman is a passenger on a ship and gives birth on board, the view to take is that nothing is owed for the child, since the fare is in any case slight and the child makes no use of the facilities provided for the passengers." (*Justinian's Digest* 19.2.19.7.)

CXXX

ON SECOND THOUGHT . . .

After the army of Carthage under the supervision of Hannibal annihilated the Roman army in the Battle of Cannae in 216 B.C., Roman commanders had to find some way of enlisting more soldiers. A promise was made, upon the eve of a battle, that freedom would be given to any slave who brought back the head of an enemy. Livy takes up this sounded-like-a-good-idea-at-the-time moment in military history:

> Nothing impeded the Romans so much as the granting of freedom in return for enemy heads. Each of the bravest fighters, as soon as he had killed one of the enemy, wasted time cutting off his head, and then, holding the head rather than his sword in the right hand, he quit the battle line, leaving the fighting to the sluggish and fainthearted. (Livy, *History of Rome* 24.15.)

"IN THE BELIEF THAT HIS SLAVES
WERE LED INTO MOST MISCHIEF
BY THEIR SEXUAL PASSIONS,
[CATO] STIPULATED THAT
THE MALES SHOULD CONSORT
WITH THE FEMALES AT A FIXED
PRICE [PAYABLE TO HIM], BUT
SHOULD NEVER APPROACH ANY
OTHER WOMAN." (PLUTARCH,
LIFE OF THE ELDER CATO 21.)

Not Exactly What I Meant To Say

Pupius Piso, the orator, not wishing to be troubled, ordered his slaves to speak only in answer to questions and not a word more. Subsequently, wishing to pay honor to Clodius [Publius Clodius Pulcher] when he was a magistrate, Piso gave orders that he be invited to dinner and prepared what was, we may suppose, a sumptuous banquet. When the hour came, the other guests were present, but Clodius was still expected, and Piso repeatedly sent the slave who regularly carried invitations to see if Clodius was approaching. And when evening came and he was finally despaired of, Piso said to the slave, "See here, did you give him the invitation?"

"I did," said the slave.

"Why hasn't he come then?"

"Because he declined."

"Then why didn't you tell me at once?"

"Because you didn't ask me that." (Plutarch, *On Talkativeness* 6.18.)

Myths in the Making

" India produces one-horned horses and donkeys. Drinking vessels are made out of their horns. If anyone drinks fatal poison
from one of these, the attempt on his life does him no harm at all, for
the horn of both the horse and the donkey seems to be an antidote to
the poison." (Aelian, *On Animals* 3.41.)

This passage foreshadows the myth of the unicorn, as does Pliny's
description of the rhinoceros:

A very fierce animal called the monoceros which has the head of
the stag, the feet of the elephant, and the tail of the boar, while the
rest of the body is like that of the horse; it makes a deep lowing
noise, and has a single black horn, which projects from the middle
of its forehead, two cubits in length. (*Natural History* 8.76.)

THAT'S SOME SERIOUS BULL SH!T!

"The bonasus is found in Paeonia [Macedonia]. It has the mane of a horse but otherwise resembles a bull. It has horns that curve back so they are useless for fighting; when attacked, it runs away, while releasing a trail of dung that can cover three furlongs [1,980 feet]. Contact with the dung burns pursuers as though they had touched fire." (Pliny, *Natural History* 8.16, expanding on Aristotle, *On the Parts of Animals* 8.63a, which mentions the bonasus's manure, but not its range or caustic firepower.)

THE PLUCK OF PLUTARCH

According to Roman religious tradition, sacred chickens are used to see to whom the gods would be favorable in battle. Romans carefully watched the feeding behavior of the sacred chickens; if they accepted the grain the Romans offered, then the Romans would prevail in the upcoming battle. Cicero reported that Publius Claudius Pulcher, on the morning of the naval Battle of Drepana in 249 B.C., performed the inspection of the omens for the battle and, to his horror, discovered that the sacred chickens had refused the grain.

The crew was in a panic and Pulcher had to think of something quick—so he threw the sacred chickens overboard pledging *"Bibant, quoniam esse nolunt"* ("Let them drink, since they don't wish to eat"). Pulcher managed to escape and returned to Rome in disgrace, where he faced charges of treason—not for incompetence but because of his sacrilegious act of disposing of the sacred chickens. He was found guilty and forced into exile. (Suetonius, *Life of Tiberius 2.*)

HOT LUNCH COMING UP!

Aristocratic Romans were known for their lavish banquets and their overindulgence in wine, food, and sex, so having a room called a vomitorium, where gorged guests could purge themselves and then come back to the table for more, makes sense. But it's a common misconception. There's nothing in the existing history of Rome that mentions a room of this sort. But around the end of the fourth century A.D., Macrobius Ambrosius Theodosius notes, "The entranceways through which people enter the theater and amphitheater in droves, pouring themselves on to the seats, we call these passages vomitoria even nowadays." (*Saturnalia* 6.4.3.) So it is assumed that in ancient Rome a passage behind or below a tier of seats in an amphitheater was called a vomitorium. Some theaters today use a shortened version of the word "vomitoriums" to describe the same passageways—they are called "voms."

MASTERING THE ART OF FRENCH COOKING HAS NOTHING ON *APICIUS*

When you just don't know what to have for dinner you can always crack open the famous Roman cookbook, *Apicius* and get some great last-minute ideas—if you happen to have a flamingo thawing in your fridge.

> Remove the flamingo's entrails, wash and dress it, put it in a pot, add water, salt, dill, and a little vinegar. Parboil, then add a bunch of leeks and coriander. When it is nearly cooked, add some winelees to give it color. Crush pepper, cumin, coriander, asafetida root, mint, and rue, add a little vinegar, dates, and the gravy from the bird. Strain it into the same pot, bind the gravy with starch, pour it over the bird, and serve. The same method is used for cooking parrots. (*Apicius*, 6.)

MESSAGES
FROM THE PAST VI

Graffiti from Pompeii, collected and recorded in the *Corpus Inscriptionum Latinarum*. The number represents the catalog number (not the date) in volume 4.

The following were all found in a basilica, or public building:

◎ 1808: "Auge loves Allotenus."

◎ 1811: "A small problem gets larger if you ignore it."

◎ 1816: "Epaphra, you are bald!"

◎ 1820: "Chie, I hope your hemorrhoids rub together so much that they hurt worse than when they ever have before!"

◎ 1824: "Let everyone in love come and see. I want to break Venus's ribs with clubs and cripple the goddess's loins. If she can strike through my soft chest, then why can't I smash her head with a club?"

◎ 1826: "Phileros is a eunuch!"

◎ 1837: "If you are able, but not willing, why do you put off our joy and kindle hope and tell me always to come back tomorrow? So, force me to die since you force me to live without you. Your gift will be to stop torturing me. Certainly, hope returns to the lover what it has once snatched away."

◎ 1842: "Gaius Pumidius Dipilus was here on October 3rd."

POLITICS AS USUAL

Quintus Tullius Cicero (102–43 B.C.) was the younger brother of the celebrated statesman Marcus Tullius Cicero. When Marcus decided to run for consul of the Roman Republic in 64 B.C., Quintus, was, well, basically his campaign manager. Quintus wrote a small book called *Commentariolum petitionis* ("Little Handbook on Electioneering"). The following passage (13) sounds like it could apply to any contemporary political race:

> Make sure that your election campaign is one long parade, magnificent and splendid, appealing to popular taste, presenting a grand and dignified spectacle. If at all possible, you should also arrange for some scandal to be stirred up against your competitors, involving either criminal behavior of sex or bribery, depending on their character.

MAY I HAVE THE ENVELOPE, PLEASE?

Cato the Younger and Julius Caesar were political enemies . . . and they didn't like each other personally, either. Cato believed that Caesar was plotting against him, and during a heated debate a note was brought from the outside and handed to Caesar. Cato thought that the note contained proof of the Catilinarian conspiracy (Lucius Sergius Catilina was refused the position of consul and then tried to form a revolt against Rome) and demanded that Caesar hand it over so he could read it. When Cato opened the letter he was embarrassed to find that it was basically a love letter to Caesar from Cato's own sister Servilia. Cato threw it to Caesar, saying, "Take it, thou sot," and then resumed his speech. (Plutarch, *Life of Brutus* 5, *Life of Cato the Younger* 24).

CXLI

THE QUEEN OF HEARTS

There's always been debate about whether Cleopatra was beautiful or plain, but one thing is certain: She was incredibly smart. Cleopatra knew the importance of making a good impression and, unlike the other Ptolemaic rulers of Egypt who did not try to learn the Egyptian language, she learned to speak fluently in the language of the Egyptians, Ethiopians, Troglodytes, Jews, Arabs, Syrians, Medes, and Parthians. Plutarch said of Cleopatra:

> For her beauty, as we are told, was in itself not altogether incomparable, nor such as to strike those who saw her; but converse with her had an irresistible charm, and her presence, combined with the persuasiveness of her discourse and the character which was somehow diffused about her behavior toward others, had something stimulating about it. (*Life of Antony* 27.)

SOUND THE TRUMPET

Roman author Claudius Aelianus (A.D. 175–235) related a story of gluttony in book 1 of his *Varia historia*, chapter 26, entitled "Of Aglais a Great Eater":

> I have heard of a woman that could sound a Trumpet, which art was her way of living, by name *Aglais*, daughter of *Megacles*; she wore a Periwig and a plume on her head, as *Posidippus* relates. At one meal she did devour twelve pounds of flesh, and four Choenixes [loaves] of bread, and drank a Congius [nine pints] of wine.

CXLIII

THE PHRASE THAT PAYS

*S*ic semper tyrannis is Latin for "thus always to tyrants." The phrase is attributed to the most famous figure in the March 15, 44 B.C. assassination of Julius Caesar, Marcus Junius Brutus (or, more commonly, Brutus). John Wilkes Booth shouted *"Sic semper tyrannis!"* after jumping from the president's box at Ford's Theatre shortly after assassinating President Lincoln on April 14, 1865. Booth used this phrase for the same reason Brutus used it (interestingly, John Wilkes Booth's father was named Junius Brutus Booth). When the Oklahoma City bomber Timothy McVeigh was arrested on April 19, 1995, he was wearing a T-shirt with *Sic semper tyrannis* and a picture of Lincoln printed on it.

CXLIV

THE SEAL OF THE
COMMONWEALTH OF VIRGINIA
SHOWS VIRTUE, SPEAR IN
HAND, DAGGER SHEATHED,
WITH HER FOOT ON TYRANNY,
WHOSE CROWN LIES NEAR HIS
DEFEATED, PROSTRATE, BODY.
AN OLD JOKE IN VIRGINIA,
GOING BACK AT LEAST AS FAR
AS THE CIVIL WAR, IS THAT *SIC
SEMPER TYRANNIS* ON THE
SEAL ACTUALLY MEANS "GET
YOUR FOOT OFF MY NECK."

INTERMINGLING AND ROMAN AROUND

Roman legions, under the command of Marcus Licinius Crassus, advanced to Parthia (now a region of Iran) during the Battle of Carrhae in 53 b.c., but were sorely defeated. Crassus's army consisted primarily of infantry (foot soldiers) and they weren't trained to fight against the swift and accurate archers in the Parthian cavalry. A great number of Roman soldiers were taken prisoner, and when a truce was called and an exchange of prisoners agreed upon there was one thing missing—all of Crassus's soldiers. Because of delays in the exchange, Parthian warriors beheaded Crassus and killed thousands of Roman soldiers. Historians believe that the Roman legion that went unaccounted for had actually escaped and were captured by Chinese forces. According to an article in the *Telegraph*, scientists believe that Liqian, China (where residents have Roman features, light eyes, and blond hair), was founded by the lost legions of Rome.("Battle of Carrhae," UNRV.com; *Telegraph*, November 23, 2010.)

ROMAN WEDDINGS

I n some marriage ceremonies, the officiator of the wedding might say "If there be any among you who know of any reason why these two should not be joined together in holy matrimony, speak now, or forever hold your peace." This is the pivotal scene in many romantic comedies, but in ancient Rome they didn't ask people if they objected —they usually asked a sheep. To see if the gods were favorable to a union a priest called a "haruspex" would sacrifice an animal—usually a sheep or chicken—and examine the entrails, particularly the liver. If there were markings or discoloration on the right side of the liver, the ceremony went forward. But if there were markings or discoloration on the left side, the Romans took that as a bad omen and the wedding was canceled or postponed.

IT WAS THE HARUSPEX SPURINNA WHO WARNED JULIUS CAESAR TO BEWARE THE IDES OF MARCH, MARCH 15, THE DATE OF CAESAR'S ASSASSINATION. "IDES" MEANS "HALF DIVISION" SO THE PHRASE "IDES OF MARCH" BASICALLY MEANS THE MIDDLE OF MARCH. "WHEN HE WAS OFFERING SACRIFICE, THE SOOTHSAYER SPURINNA WARNED HIM TO BEWARE OF DANGER, WHICH WOULD COME NOT LATER THAN THE IDES OF MARCH." (SUETONIUS, *LIVES OF THE CAESARS* 81.)

STUPID
ANCIENT
HISTORY

WHY SO CROSS?

"While governing in Sicily [in 97 B.C.], Lucius Domitius Ahenobarbus showed that he had a very determined character. When an extraordinarily large wild boar was brought to him, he ordered the shepherd who had killed it to be summoned and asked him how he had killed the beast; on learning that he had used a hunting spear, he had him crucified; to root out the highway robbery which was devastating the province, he himself had issued an edict forbidding the possession of weapons." (Valerius Maximus, *Memorable Deeds and Sayings* 6.3.5.)

CXLIX

HONEYMOON HIGH JINKS

"The bride's-maid, so called, took her [the captured bride] in charge, cut her hair off close to the head, put a man's cloak and sandals on her, and laid her down on a pallet, on the floor, alone, in the dark. Then the bride-groom, not flown with wine nor enfeebled by excesses [impotent], but composed and sober, after supping at his public mess-table as usual, slipped stealthily into the room where the bride lay, loosed her virgin's zone, and bore her in his arms to the marriage bed. Then, after spending a short time with his bride, he went away composedly to his usual quarters, there to sleep with the other young men. And so he continued to do from that time on, spending his days with his comrades, and sleeping with them at night, but visiting his bride by stealth and with every precaution." (Plutarch, *Life of Lycurgus* 15.3.4.)

After a few more days like this, the bride was taken back to her parents' house, and the marriage was considered legal and complete.

ENGAGEMENT AND WEDDING
RINGS ARE WORN ON THE
FOURTH FINGER OF THE
LEFT HAND BECAUSE IT WAS
ONCE BELIEVED THAT A VEIN,
VENA AMORIS ("VEIN OF
LOVE"), IN THAT FINGER LED
DIRECTLY TO THE HEART.

A Pot to Piss In

Chamber pots in ancient Roman times were not all unisex; the chamber pot referred to as a *matella* was for gentlemen, and a boat-shaped *scaphium* was for ladies. All houses, rich and poor, had chamber pots and, at that time, before the understanding of the bacteria and diseases that are caused by poor sanitation, Romans would traditionally empty their chamber pots out of their windows. This became such a hazard for people on the street that a law called the *Dejecti Effusive Actio* was eventually passed, which fined a person who threw or poured anything out of an open window and hit someone. The law awarded damages to the injured party but applied only during daytime hours. (John Murray, *A Dictionary of Greek and Roman Antiquities* [London: 1875], p. 388.)

THE LATIN TERM *PLUMBUS* MEANS "LEAD," AND IT IS WHERE WE GET THE WORDS "PLUMBING" AND "PLUMBER." A "PLUMB BOB," THE WEIGHT AT THE END OF A LINE USED IN CONSTRUCTION AND SURVEYING, IS ALSO DERIVED FROM *PLUMBUS*.

BEARING FALSE WITNESS III

"God helps those who help themselves" is a popular phrase batted around by people who also ascribe to the "Pull yourself up by your own bootstraps" mentality. (I never figured out how one could pull oneself up in such a manner.) Anyway, this phrase isn't found anywhere in the Bible and, in fact, it goes against every tenet taught in both the Old and New Testament, especially contradicting the teachings of Jesus. The phrase originated in ancient Greece and can be found as the moral of the Aesop fable "Hercules and the Waggoner" (sixth century B.C.).

This is what the Bible really says about self-reliance:

"The LORD is close to the brokenhearted and saves those who are crushed in spirit." (Psalm 34:18 New International Version.)

"This is what the LORD says: 'Cursed is the one who trusts in man, who draws strength from mere flesh and whose heart turns away from the LORD.'" (Jeremiah 17:5 NIV.)

"Those who trust themselves are fools, but those who walk in wisdom are kept safe." (Proverbs 28:26 NIV.)

You're in Fashion

The mean remark "I wouldn't pee in your mouth if your teeth were on fire" didn't hold true with the Romans. The Romans frequently used urine as a mouthwash and tooth whitener. But being Romans they wouldn't use just anyone's urine; in fact, they never used urine of other Romans. No, they got their pee from Portugal. (Four out of five dentists recommend Portuguese urine for their patients who use urine.) Portuguese urine was thought to be more potent—had a higher pH, if you will—than Roman urine. Because urine contains ammonia and urea, which kills germs, it would have helped fight gingivitis. I'm not sure if it freshened breath, though.

AS CHILDREN, SPARTAN MALES WERE TRAINED AT AN EARLY AGE TO BE TOUGH AND RESOURCEFUL. THEY WERE NOT ALLOWED TO WEAR CLOTHES AND WERE INTENTIONALLY STARVED TO ENCOURAGE THEM TO BE CRAFTY AND STEAL FOOD. IF THEY WERE APPREHENDED THEY WERE SORELY PUNISHED, BUT NOT FOR THE ACT OF THEFT—FOR GETTING CAUGHT.

WORMING THEIR WAY INTO HISTORY

What the Greeks don't take credit for creating, the Chinese can—paper, gunpowder, the compass, and so forth. They also discovered how to make silk from the cocoons of the silkworm about five thousand years ago. (How they ever figured this out is beyond me.) It was such a luxury item that it was available only to the emperors of China, but soon demand for the amazing fabric spread throughout the known world. It was very costly, and the less fortunate who couldn't afford it came up with a knockoff variety. They discovered that if they softened cotton by beating it with a stick and then rubbed the fibers against a stone, it would shine like silk; the garments they made from the shiny cotton looked and felt close to silk. The Sanskrit word for the fabric was *citra*, meaning "shiny," then Hindi *ch nt*, and from that the word became "chintz." In today's language, "chintzy" means something that is of poor quality and cheap. So, once again, the Chinese leave their mark on the world.

ROMAN EMPEROR TITUS
FLAVIUS CAESAR VESPASIANUS
AUGUSTUS, KNOWN AS
VESPASIAN, RULED FROM A.D.
NOVEMBER 17, 69, TO JUNE
23, 79, AND WAS KNOWN FOR
HAVING A VERY STERN LOOK.
"VESPASIAN HAD RATHER
STRAINED FACIAL FEATURES.
HE ONCE CHALLENGED
SOMEONE TO SAY SOMETHING
FUNNY AT HIS EXPENSE, AND
THE JOKER REPLIED RATHER
WITTILY, 'I WILL, ONCE
YOU'VE FINISHED RELIEVING
YOURSELF.'" (SUETONIUS,
LIFE OF VESPASIAN 20.)

PTOLEMY PLACE

This is from a papyrus letter submitted to the royal court in Egypt in the pre-Roman period explaining the dramatic details of a wrongful and malicious act.

> Greeting to King Ptolemy. I have been wronged by a woman named Psenobastis from Pysa. I went to Pysa on business. She leaned out of an upper-story window and drenched me by emptying a chamber pot into the street. When I complained angrily, she pulled at my cloak, exposing my chest, and spat in my face. I can provide witnesses to prove that I have been subjected to this unjust attack. (*Lille Papyri* 2.24.)

BURNIN' DOWN THE HOUSE

The Greek historian Thucydides (460–395 B.C.), in his book *The History of the Peloponnesian War*, describes the creation and use of the first flamethrower during a military battle. The Peloponnesian War was fought between Athens and Sparta from 431 to 404 B.C., and during the Battle of Delium in 424 B.C., the Athenians had built a fort made of wood and vines and were holding their position against the Spartans. The Spartans soon grew tired of waiting and devised an "engine" by splitting and hollowing out a timber, putting an iron pipe inside, putting the timber back together, and securing it with iron bands. They "hung by chains a cauldron at one extremity," filled the cauldron with "lighted coals, sulfur, and pitch," and then "inserted huge bellows into their end of the beam and blew with them." Using this primitive but effective flamethrower, the Spartans burned down the Athenians' fort and were victorious. During the Byzantine Empire of the Middle Ages they called their flamethrower "Greek fire" in homage to the Spartans. (Thucydides, *The History of the Peloponnesian War* 4.9.)

DON'T BE SO SPONTANEOUS

Flies lay their eggs in nasty things, such as rotting animal corpses. When the eggs hatch, little fly babies, called maggots, come crawling out. Modern science is very familiar now with the process by which a larva develops into an adult insect, but in ancient times they believed that maggots were a by-product of dead animals or corpses. They called this process "spontaneous generation" or "equivocal generation," and none other than the great Aristotle (384–322 B.C.) synthesized the hypothesis. "So with animals," wrote Aristotle, "some spring from parent animals according to their kind, whilst others grow spontaneously and not from kindred stock; and of these instances of spontaneous generation some come from putrefying earth or vegetable matter, as is the case with a number of insects, while others are spontaneously generated in the inside of animals out of the secretions of their several organs." (Aristotle, *History of Animals* 5.1.) Astonishingly, this theory of spontaneous generation held sway until as late as the nineteenth century.

"WHEN PEOPLE UNWITTINGLY EAT HUMAN FLESH, SERVED BY UNSCRUPULOUS RESTAURANT OWNERS AND OTHER SUCH PEOPLE, THE SIMILARITY TO PORK IS OFTEN NOTED." (GALEN, *ON THE POWER OF FOODS* 3.)

THE BIRDS AND THE BEES

Although Aristotle was a student of Plato, a teacher of Alexander the Great, and an all-around great thinker, he also had a few odd ideas. He believed mice magically formed from piles of dirty hay and that the morning dew created plant lice. He thought that shelled mollusks formed in mud, clams and scallops in sand, oysters in slime, and the barnacle and the limpet in the hollows of rocks. (Aristotle, *The History of Animals* 5.15.)

Parasitic worms called "ascarids" were formed on "the slime of wells," and "the tick is generated from couch-grass." He also deduced that reddish worms came from old drifts of snow, and some species of grub worm was believed to grow out of fire. (Aristotle, *The History of Animals* 5.19).

CLX

"PEOPLE WHO DRINK WINE
IN WHICH EELS HAVE BEEN
DROWNED LOSE THEIR APPETITE
FOR DRINKING WINE." (SAINT
ISIDORE, *ETYMOLOGIES* 12.6.41.)

AHEAD BY A NOSE

Believe it or not, plastic surgery has been around for nearly three thousand years. Reconstructive surgery techniques were being carried out in India by 800 B.C. Suśruta, the father of surgery, in his book the *Suśruta saṃhitā*, describes more than 300 surgical procedures and 120 surgical instruments and created eight classifications of human surgery. Suśruta was also known to have developed a procedure to repair noses that had been cut off as a punishment for adultery—the first rhinoplasty (Greek: *rhis*, "nose," plus *plassein*, "to shape").

CLXII

CORNELIUS FIDUS, WHO WAS MARRIED TO THE POET OVID'S STEPDAUGHTER, ONCE BURST INTO TEARS IN THE SENATE WHEN GNAEUS DOMITIUS CORBULO (A.D. 7–67), NERO'S GREAT GENERAL AND BROTHER-IN-LAW OF THE EMPEROR CALIGULA, CALLED HIM A *STRUTHOCAMELUS DEPILATUS*, OR "PLUCKED OSTRICH." (SENECA, *ON THE CONSTANCY OF THE WISE MAN* 17.1.)

You Shouldn't Swear

ippocrates (460–377 B.C.) is regarded as the father of modern medicine and the first doctor to reject the prevailing superstitious belief that illness was caused by the gods. He's probably best known in modern times as the man who created the Hippocratic oath—you know, "First, to do no harm." Well, the Hippocratic oath is fairly lengthy so I'm not going to write it all here. But here are a couple of interesting excerpts:

> "I will not give a fatal draught to anyone if I am asked, nor will I suggest any such thing. Neither will I give a woman means to procure an abortion.

> "I will not abuse my position to indulge in sexual contacts with the bodies of women or of men, whether they be freemen or slaves."

The Hippocratic oath says doctors are not supposed to perform euthanasia or abortion, or sleep with their patients, so how can modern-day doctors do those things? Quite simply, they take a different oath—there are four other versions of a physician's oath, each tailor-made to suit different needs.

MESSAGES
FROM THE PAST VII

Graffiti from Pompeii, collected and recorded in the *Corpus Inscriptionum Latinarum*. The number represents the catalog number (not the date) in volume 4:

The following were all found in a basilica, or public building:

◎ 1852: Pyrrhus to his colleague Chius: "I grieve because I hear you have died; and so farewell."

◎ 1863: "Take hold of your servant girl whenever you want to; it's your right."

◎ 1864: "Samius to Cornelius: Go hang yourself!"

◎ 1880: "Lucius Istacidius, I regard as a stranger anyone who doesn't invite me to dinner."

◎ 1880: "The man I am having dinner with is a barbarian."

◎ 1881: "Virgula to her friend Tertius: You are disgusting!"

◎ 1882: "The one who buggers a fire burns his penis."

◎ 1904: "O walls, you have held up so much tedious graffiti that I am amazed that you have not already collapsed in ruin."

◎ 1926: "Epaphra is not good at ballgames."

◎ 1928: "Love dictates to me as I write and Cupid shows me the way, but may I die if god should wish me to go on without you."

YOU'RE PULLING MY LEG

"No one now believes in the existence of the Hydra of Lerna [killed by Hercules as one of his twelve labors] or of the three-headed Chimaera, but the amphisbaena is a snake with a head at both ends. When it is going forward, it uses one head as a tail, the other as a head, and when it is going backward, it uses its heads in the opposite manner." (Aelian, *On Animals* 9.23.)

CLXVI

SCIRE EX VOBIS VOLO, OVUMNE PRIUS EXSTITERIT AN GALLINA: "I WANT TO KNOW FROM YOU WHETHER THE EGG CAME FIRST OR THE CHICKEN." (MACROBIUS, *SATURNALIA* 7.16, EARLY FIFTH CENTURY.)

A PLEDGE DRIVE

In a survey of the Hippocratic oaths taken in 150 U.S. and Canadian medical schools in 1993, it was found that only 14 percent of modern oaths disallowed euthanasia, 11 percent held covenant with a deity, 8 percent forswore abortion, and only 3 percent banned sexual contact with patients. (R. D. Orr, et al., "Use of the Hippocratic Oath: A Review of Twentieth-Century Practice and a Content Analysis of Oaths Administered in Medical Schools in the U.S. and Canada in 1993," *Journal of Clinical Ethics* 8 [Winter 1997]: 377–88.)

CLXVIII

"WHEN POMPEY ATTEMPTED TO ENTER ROME IN A TRIUMPHAL PROCESSION IN A CHARIOT DRAWN BY FOUR ELEPHANTS, IT GOT STUCK IN THE CITY GATE." (PLUTARCH, *LIFE OF POMPEY* 14.)

What's in a Name?

Although Julius Caesar himself was not born by caesarean section, there does seem to be a link between the two names. It's possible that the name "Caesar" may have become the family cognomen because one of Caesar's relatives was born by caesarean. In fact, Pliny the Elder refers to a Caesar (an ancestor of the dictator) as being so born: "The first, too, of the Caesars was so named, from his having been removed by an incision in his mother's womb." (Pliny, *Natural History* 2.7.9.)

Or the family name may have had nothing to do with the caesarean section. Instead, it may have come from an ancestor who was born with a full head of hair, from *caesaries*, meaning "mane" or "luxuriant hair"; or one who had blue-gray eyes, from *caesius*, meaning "blue-gray;" or from *caesai*, the Moorish or Punic word for "elephant." In fact, during his reign, Julius Caesar had coins struck with an image of an elephant above the name Caesar. Guess it's a better image than the whole "getting cut out of the womb" alternative.

Looks Can Be Deceiving

The "doctrine of signatures" is a diagnostic system rooted in antiquity and based on the simple principle that the creator gave us clues as to what plants might be curative because their shape would resemble the part of the body they were designed to cure. For example, walnuts were believed to be good for the brain because the meat of the walnut looks like a brain and is encased in a hard shell, not unlike the human skull. The doctrine of signatures was the major diagnostic and prescriptive theory and was practiced by preeminent doctors such as Pedanius Dioscorides (A.D. 40–90) and Galen of Pergamum (A.D. 129–200), and it remained a central plank of medical thinking until as recently as the late nineteenth century.

ALL IN THE NAME OF GOOD HEALTH

In the doctrine of signatures, not only did some plants look like the area on the human they were supposed to help, they were also given easily identifiable names, such as lousewort, to repel lice; hedge woundwort, thought to have antiseptic qualities; and the easier to figure out spleenwort, liverwort, toothwort, and lungwort. Occasionally they got something right. St. John's wort, for example, is still used for the treatment of depression. Then again, some times they got it very wrong. Because the shape of its seeds looked like a human jaw, henbane was recommended for toothache, but henbane is a poisonous hallucinogen that can be fatal. I guess it would qualify as taking care of the toothache, though.

THE ROMANS INCORPORATED
THE GREEK BELIEF THAT GOATS
BREATHE THROUGH THEIR
EARS. VARRO CONFIRMS
THIS IN *ON AGRICULTURE*
(2.3) AS DOES PLINY IN
NATURAL HISTORY (8.202).

STUPID
ANCIENT
HISTORY

RHINE TIME

The Romans were so focused in their continuing battles with the Goths that they made the mistake of removing guards from their borders and sending them to the front. The Vandals finally got the break they were looking for when in A.D. 406, during an unusually cold winter, the Rhine River froze, and they were able to cross over into Roman territory. Once there they totally devastated the Gauls and settled in for the big fight. They bided their time and in A.D. 455 went on to sack Rome; the Vandals not only took Rome, they also took Empress Licinia Eudoxia and her daughters Eudocia and Placidia. The Vandals were on a roll and went on to conquer northern Africa, taking the city of Carthage and establishing a kingdom that lasted for only a century before again being conquered by the Romans. The English word "vandal" comes from these people and, unsurprisingly, means a person who wrecks things.

JULIUS CAESAR WAS NEVER AN EMPEROR. ROME WAS STILL A REPUBLIC IN HIS DAY (UP UNTIL THE VERY END, THAT IS), AND CAESAR HELPED TO BRING ABOUT THE REPUBLIC'S FALL.

THE IDES OF MARCH

Most of us know that Brutus and a bunch of other toga-wearing radicals stabbed Julius Caesar to death but don't really know the reason behind the assassination. Julius Caesar was dictator of the Roman Republic at the time and was keen on shifting the power balance over to one person—himself—and making Rome an empire instead of a republic. He had recently been declared *dictator perpetuo* ("dictator in perpetuity"), an office he held from either January 26 or February 15, 44 B.C., until his death on March 15 of that year. Sixty Roman senators who called themselves Liberators, led by Gaius Cassius Longinus and Marcus Junius Brutus, thought by killing Caesar they could return Rome back to a republic. So on the Ides of March (March 15), 44 B.C., the Liberators accosted Julius Caesar as he was passing the Theatre of Pompey on his way to the Senate, stabbing him twenty-three times until he died. The actions of the Liberators threw Rome into chaos and led to civil war. After two years of infighting, Caesar's supporters, led by his general Mark Antony and Caesar's eighteen-year-old adopted son, Octavius, established a permanent Roman Empire. Brutus committed suicide after losing the Battle of Philippi in Greece in 42 B.C. (Plutarch, *Life of Caesar* 66; Suetonius *Life of the Caesars, Julius* 82.)

CAN I BE FRANK?

The barbarian horde, known to the Romans as the Franks, occupied the area north and east of the Rhine (right outside the Roman border). Their first kingdom, called Francia, lasted from the third to the tenth century in what is now eastern Europe. The first great king of the Franks was Clovis I, who was responsible for conquering even more land in Europe, extending to what is now Spain. Outsiders eventually conquered the Franks, and their rule ended around the turn of the first millennium. They did leave one thing behind, however: the name "Francia," which means "country of the Franks," which gave rise to the country we know today as France. Clovis I was such a beloved leader that for centuries following his death many French kings paid homage to him by using a variation of his name—Louis.

YOU GOTH TO BE KIDDING

The Goths, a name given to this barbarian tribe by the Romans, lived just across the Danube River from the Roman Empire in A.D. 376. The Goths were in fear of being invaded by the Huns, and they pleaded with the Romans to allow them to enter their territory. Roman emperor Valens gave them permission and sent a fleet of boats to systematically bring tens of thousands of Goths across the Danube to safety. Valens didn't do it completely out of the goodness of his heart; he said he would let the Goths live in the Roman Empire if they promised to serve in the Roman army. That seemed like a good idea at the time but eventually Alaric I, a Gothic general in the Roman army, led the first sack of Rome, in A.D. 410.

"AFTER GRAZING ALL NIGHT ON LAND, TURTLES GO BACK TO THE SEA AT DAWN, FULL BUT TIRED. THEY DOZE OFF ON THE SURFACE OF THE WATER, AND THEIR SNORING GIVES THEIR LOCATION AWAY TO HUNTERS." (PLINY, *NATURAL HISTORY* 9.36.)

TOSS ANOTHER ONE ON THE FIRE

There are a lot of rumors and weird mummy facts out there; some are true and some are false. One that is still circulating, but is patently false, is that mummies were so abundant that Egyptian railroads used them as fuel to power their locomotives. It seems so absurd that it must be true, because who would make up such a thing? Well, I'll tell you who. It was humorist Mark Twain. In his 1869 book, *The Innocents Abroad: or, The New Pilgrim's Progress*, he wrote:

> I shall not speak of the railway, for it is like any other railway—I shall only say that the fuel they use for the locomotive is composed of mummies three thousand years old, purchased by the ton or by the graveyard for that purpose, and that sometimes one hears the profane engineer call out pettishly, "D——n these plebeians, they don't burn worth a cent—pass out a King."

So it sounds like they used mummies for fuel, until you read the next line written with a wink of the eye: "Stated to me for a fact. I only tell it as I got it. I am willing to believe it. I can believe anything." Apparently, Twain's not the only one who will believe anything.

ARISTOTLE WROTE 170 BOOKS ("CHAPTERS" IN MODERN TERMS), 47 OF WHICH SURVIVED.

THAT'S SO GOTH

So, what's the difference between a Visigoth and an Ostrogoth, apart from the way they're spelled? Both are names for barbarian hordes (according to the Romans). The Visigoths entered Roman territory in the late fourth century; the Ostrogoths entered around the fifth century. After Romulus Augustulus, the last western Roman emperor, was deposed in A.D. 476, barbarian groups set up kingdoms in what used to be the Roman Empire. The Visigoths settled in Spain and occupied it until A.D. 711, and the Ostrogoths, under Theodoric the Great, established a kingdom in Italy in the late fifth century.

The Goths give their name to the word "gothic," which initially meant barbarous, crude, or uncouth. From there the word spread to include gothic fiction/horror (gothicism's origin is attributed to English author Horace Walpole, with his 1764 novel *The Castle of Otranto*, subtitled *A Gothic Story*); gothic music (Bauhaus was an English rock band formed in Northampton in 1978 and are generally considered the first gothic rock group), the subculture goths, and so forth.

THE ROMAN EMPIRE STARTED WITH ROMULUS AND
REMUS AND ENDED WITH ROMULUS AUGUSTULUS.

THE HAPPY HOOKER

She was the most successful and sought-after courtesan in ancient Greece and her name was Phryne (fourth century B.C.). When she was born her parents called her Mnesarete (Greek for "virtue"), but because her complexion was yellowish, she was called Phryne (Greek for "toad") by the other courtesans. Still, the men loved her and soon Phryne was commanding one hundred times the going rate for her services. She became so wealthy that she offered to pay out of her own pocket to have the walls of Thebes rebuilt, which had been laid to ruin by Alexander the Great (336 B.C.), on the condition that the words "Destroyed by Alexander, restored by Phryne the courtesan," were inscribed upon them. Her offer was rejected. (Athenaeus, *Deipnosophistae* 13.589–599.)

EXPOSING THE TRUTH

round 340 B.C., Phryne the courtesan was accused of upsetting the gods by appearing nude during the festival of Poseidon at Eleusis. According to Athenaeus (*Deipnosophistae* 13.585), the renowned Greek painter Apelles got his inspiration for his masterpiece *Venus anadyomene* (*Venus Rising from the Sea*) from Phryne's act. At her trial, the orator Hyperides, her defender and also one of her lovers, tore open Phryne's robe and exposed her naked breasts to the court. It was all part of his legal defense. He concluded that if she was, in fact, the most beautiful woman in Athens then she must have been a favorite of Aphrodite, goddess of love and beauty. And if a god likes her—no man should judge her. It worked, too. The panel of judges ruled in Phryne's favor. (Athenaeus, *Deipnosophistae* 13.591e.)

ACCORDING TO PLINY THE ELDER, THE MOST AMAZING BELIEF ABOUT HYENAS IS THEIR ABILITY TO IMITATE HUMAN SPEECH. IT WAS KNOWN THAT HYENAS WOULD STALK AROUND THE SHEPHERD'S HUT AND LEARN ONE OF THEIR NAMES— THEN AT NIGHT THEY WOULD CALL TO HIM AND DEVOUR HIM WHEN HE ANSWERED. (*NATURAL HISTORY* 8.106.) HE ALSO REPORTS THE BELIEF (28.100) THAT IF YOU PLACE A HYENA'S TONGUE BETWEEN THE SOLE OF YOUR FOOT AND YOUR SHOE YOU WILL NOT BE BARKED AT BY DOGS.

You've Come a Long Way, Baby I

From humble beginnings, Theodora (A.D. 497–548), daughter of Acacius, a bear trainer of the hippodrome's Green faction in Constantinople, rose to great prominence. Upon the death of her father, Theodora was forced by her actress-dancer mother into a life in the theater and then of prostitution. (Claudine M. Dauphin, "Brothels, Baths and Babes: Prostitution in the Byzantine Holy Land," *Classics Ireland* 3 [1996]: pp. 47–72.) At sixteen, Theodora became the mistress to a Syrian official named Hecebolus, and in A.D. 522 she caught the eye of Justinian I, the emperor Justin I's nephew. Justinian was so enamored that he wanted to marry Theodora, but Byzantine law forbade royals from marrying beneath their station (and an actress and prostitute was as beneath as one could get). Seeing his nephew so smitten, and being the emperor, Justin I simply changed the law, and Justinian and Theodora became husband and wife.

CLXXXIV

MESSAGES
FROM THE PAST VIII

Graffiti from Pompeii, collected and recorded in the *Corpus Inscriptionum Latinarum*. The number after the location in parentheses is the catalog number of the inscription (not the date) in volume 4:

- (Inn of the Mule Drivers; left of the door) 4957: "We have wet the bed, host. I confess we have done wrong. If you want to know why, there was no chamber pot."

- (Atrium of the House of the Jews) 2409a: "Stronius Stronnius knows nothing!"

- (House of Curvius Marcellus and Fabia; in the tablinum) 4993: "Ampliatus Pedania is a thief!"

- (House of Poppaeus Sabinus; peristyle) 5092: "If you felt the fires of love, mule driver, you would make more haste to see Venus. I love a charming boy; I ask you, goad the mules; let's go. Take me to Pompeii, where love is sweet. You are mine."

- (House of the Centenary; in the atrium) 5213: "My lusty son, with how many women have you had sexual relations?"

- (House of the Centenary; in the latrine near the front door) 5243: "Secundus defecated here," written three times on one wall.

- (House of the Centenary; interior of the house) 5279: "Once you are dead, you are nothing."

YOU'VE COME A LONG WAY, BABY II

Justinian I, commonly known as Justinian the Great, became emperor of the Byzantine Empire in A.D. 527. He and his wife, Theodora, ruled during a prosperous time and were much loved by their subjects. Theodora turned out to be more than just a beautiful and loving wife; she was also a gifted politician, helping to create a new constitution to curb corruption, expanding women's rights in divorce, shutting down houses of ill repute, and establishing convents for former prostitutes. When she died on June 28, 548, at around age fifty, she became known as the most influential and powerful woman in the empire's 1,100-year history. Theodora went from actress to a prostitute to empress, and, eventually, like her husband, became a saint in the Orthodox Church (commemorated on November 14).

"BIRDS IMITATE THE HUMAN VOICE, AND PARROTS CAN ACTUALLY CONDUCT A CONVERSATION....THEY ARE PARTICULARLY RISQUÉ IF THEY DRINK WINE." (PLINY, *NATURAL HISTORY* 10.117.)

PLINY OF QUESTIONS

P liny the Elder (Gaius Plinius Secundus), Roman author, historian, naturalist, and natural philosopher, died in the summer of A.D. 79, while attempting to rescue his friend Rectina and her family from the eruption of Mount Vesuvius, which had just obliterated the cities of Pompeii and Herculaneum. At this time in his life, Pliny was serving as prefect of the Roman navy, upon appointment from Vespasian. On the day of the eruption of Mount Vesuvius, Pliny was stationed at Misenum and was preparing to cross the Bay of Naples to observe the phenomenon directly. After getting the letter of distress, Pliny boarded a small cutter and landed on the shore of Herculaneum. He found his friend and her party and loaded them into the ship, but he himself was too exhausted to continue. They found Pliny's body three days later covered in pumice but with no apparent external injuries. It was a sad end to one of the greatest minds of the ancient world. (Jacob Bigelow, MD, "Death of Pliny the Elder," *Littell's Living Age* 61 [April, May, June 1859]: pp. 123–25; Pliny the Younger *Letters* "LXV. To Tacitus.")

In Name Only

Pliny the Elder is still remembered through classifications used in volcanology (the study of volcanoes). The term "Plinian eruption" (or "Vesuvian eruption") refers to a very violent eruption of a volcano marked by columns of smoke and ash extending high into the stratosphere. The term "ultra-Plinian" is reserved for the most violent type of Plinian eruptions. On the Smithsonian Institution's Volcanic Explosivity Index, a VEI of 6 to 8 is classified as ultra-Plinian, with ash plumes more than sixteen miles high and erupted material of 200 cubic miles or more. Eruptions in the ultra-Plinian category include Lake Toba (estimated 75,000 B.C.), Tambora (April 1815), and Krakatoa (August 26–27, 1883).

CLXXXVIII

"A SLAVE IS NOT DISEASED IF HE
WETS HIS BED WHILE DRUNK
AND ASLEEP OR BECAUSE
HE IS TOO LAZY TO GET UP.
IF, HOWEVER, HE CANNOT
RETAIN HIS URINE BECAUSE
OF A DEFECTIVE BLADDER,
HIS SALE MAY BE CANCELED
BECAUSE OF THAT DEFECT. IT
CANNOT BE CANCELED SIMPLY
BECAUSE HE WETS HIS BED."
(JUSTINIAN'S DIGEST 21.1.14.1.)

THE MIDAS TOUCH

I n Greek mythology, King Midas was the man who wished that whatever he touched would turn to gold. The legend goes that Silenus, right-hand satyr to the god Dionysus, was found passed out drunk in Midas's vineyard. He was tied up and held captive until Midas ordered him released. Dionysus was so thankful to Midas that he gave him a wish, and Midas asked for the golden touch. This didn't work out as well as expected. Midas touched his daughter and she turned to gold, and then everything he tried to eat turned to gold, and so forth. It's a great story of greed, but there really was a King Midas, and archaeologists can tell you not only that he was indeed able to eat—but also exactly what he ate.

University of Pennsylvania archaeologists discovered the tomb of King Midas, who reigned over Phrygia from about 720 to about 695 B.C., in the Turkish city of Gordion in 1957. Inside the tomb were textiles, wooden furniture, and eighty clay jars containing food residue, which usually decomposes, especially after 2,700 years. Apparently King Midas was the honorary guest at a send-off banquet, and nearly 150 people ate spicy goat or lamb stew made from meat that had been marinated in honey, wine, and olive oil. Lentils were probably eaten with flatbread as no utensils were found in the tomb. And to wash it all down archaeologists found traces of barley beer, wine, and mead (a fermented beverage made from honey, water, malt, and yeast). They also discovered drinking vessels, but not one of them was made of gold.

LET THE GAMES BEGIN

The famous Roman gladiatorial sports lasted for seven hundred years, from about 310 B.C. to the mid–fifth century. They started as a form of punishment for slaves, captured enemy soldiers, or criminals condemned to execution, who would be forced to fight one another to the death. More interesting than going to night court, the spectacle increased in popularity and eventually transformed into the event we see in movies, with a gladiator (from *gladius*, "sword") and a hapless opponent going at each other with a variety of nasty-looking weapons. As most gladiators were themselves slaves, the greatest reward was manumission (freedom), symbolized by the gift of a wooden training sword or staff (*rudis*) from an officiator of the game called an "editor." One of the greatest gladiators in history, Flamma, was awarded the *rudis* four times, but chose to remain a gladiator. His gravestone in Sicily includes his record: "Flamma, *secutor* [a class of gladiator], lived 30 years, fought 34 times, won 21 times, fought to a draw 9 times, defeated 4 times, a Syrian by nationality. Delicatus made this for his deserving comrade-in-arms." (Donald Kyle, *Spectacles of Death in Ancient Rome*, p. 112.)

THE GREAT RACE

Before it became famous as a race, Marathon was just ten square miles of open land northeast of Athens. During the summer of 490 B.C., Marathon was the scene of an epic battle in which ten thousand Greek soldiers were outnumbered two to one by the forces of the Persian army. The Greek general, Miltiades, knew he needed reinforcements and wanted the best fighters in the world to help fill his ranks. The best fighters were, of course, Spartans. The only way to communicate over long distances in that day was to send a specially trained man, called a "runner," who, as the name implies, would run to deliver the intended message. The general sent his strongest runner, Pheidippides (530–490 B.C.), to fetch some Spartans from Athens some twenty-six miles away. When Pheidippides arrived at the Spartan camp they were celebrating a religious event and couldn't come, so Pheidippides ran back to Marathon to tell the general the bad news. (Herodotus, *Histories* 6.105–6.) Miltiades waged a brilliant attack without the help of the Spartans and miraculously defeated the Persians (by Greek accounts they lost 192 men while the Persians lost more than 6,000). Miltiades again sent Pheidippides to Athens to tell of his great accomplishment. Pheidippides raced the 26 miles and 385 yards and, upon entering Athens, exclaimed "*Nike!*" (which means "victory") and then collapsed and died. The marathon is a long-distance running event with an official distance of 42.195 kilometers (26 miles and 385 yards); it seems like they should have named it the Pheidippides.

WATER TORTURE

I n 482 B.C. Xerxes I wanted to cross a narrow strait in northwestern Turkey (connecting the Aegean Sea to the Sea of Marmara) called the Hellespont (now the Dardanelles) so he could move his army from Persia into Greece. Xerxes had his soldiers prepare "ropes of papyrus and of white flax" to be used to construct the bridge. Unfortunately, Xerxes's first bridge was destroyed by a storm. He was so upset that he not only punished the bridge builders, he also punished the Hellespont. He ordered his men to whip the water three hundred times as punishment, throw in fetters (leg cuffs or shackles), and thrust in red-hot pokers. It sounds crazy, but Xerxes's second attempt to bridge the Hellespont was successful. (Herodotus, *Histories* "Polymnia" 7.35.)

IT IS CONSIDERED A BAD OMEN IF BOTH OXEN
IN A TEAM DEFECATE SIMULTANEOUSLY WHILE
YOKED. (CICERO, *ON DIVINATION* 2.77.)

WONDER OF WONDERS

We've heard about the Seven Wonders of the Ancient World, but most of us still wonder what exactly they are. Well, I'll tell you.

I   The Great Pyramid at Giza. Built by Pharaoh Khufu for his tomb around 2500 B.C. in Cairo, Egypt, this is the oldest of the seven ancient wonders and the only one that has survived the sands of time.

II   The Hanging Gardens of Babylon. Built in ancient Babylon, near present-day Baghdad, around 600 B.C. by King Nebuchadnezzar for his wife, Amyitis, who was homesick for the mountains of her native land. The terraced gardens were some seventy-five feet high and covered with trees, flowers, fountains, and waterfalls. It was a wonder for its day, but not a trace of the garden exists today.

III   The Temple of Artemis at Ephesus. Built by King Croesus, in Ephesus, near modern Selcuk, Turkey, around 550 B.C., the temple was considered the most beautiful structure on earth, made completely of marble (except the roof). It featured gold pillars and four bronze statues of Amazons, the women warriors who were Artemis's most faithful followers. Antipater of Sidon, who compiled the list of the Seven Wonders, describes the finished temple:

> I have set eyes on the wall of lofty Babylon on which is a road for chariots, and the statue of Zeus by the Alpheus, and the hanging gardens, and the colossus of the Sun, and the huge labor of the high pyramids,

and the vast tomb of Mausolus; but when I saw the house of Artemis that mounted to the clouds, those other marvels lost their brilliancy, and I said, 'Lo, apart from Olympus, the Sun never looked on aught so grand.' (Antipater, *Greek Anthology* 9.58.)

The structure was destroyed by an arsonist named Herostratus (see his story on page VIII) in 356 B.C. It was then rebuilt, and then burned down again by those pesky Goths.

IV   The Statue of Zeus. The Statue of Zeus at Olympia was made by the Greek sculptor Phidias, ca. 432 B.C., and erected in the Temple of Zeus in Olympia, Greece. The seated statue, some forty-three feet tall, occupied half of the width of the aisle of the temple built to house it. "It seems that if Zeus were to stand up," the geographer Strabo noted early in the first century B.C., "he would un-roof the temple." Zeus's body was made of ivory, and his beard, robe, and sandals were made of gold. His throne, also made of gold, was encrusted with precious stones. Zeus went to meet his maker after a fire destroyed the statue in 462 A.D.

V   The Mausoleum at Halicarnassus. Built around 353 B.C. in Halicarnassus (present Bodrum, Turkey) by Queen Artemisia in loving tribute to her husband, King Mausolus, who was also her brother. It is unknown exactly when and how the mausoleum came to ruin, but according to

Eustathius in the twelfth century on his commentary of the *Iliad*, "It was and is a wonder." We are therefore led to believe that the building was likely ruined, probably by an earthquake, between this period and 1402, when the Knights of Saint John arrived (who used many of the stones from the mausoleum to fortify their castle of Bodrum). The marble that wasn't reused for other purposes was burned into lime. (James Fergusson, *The Mausoleum at Halicarnassus Restored in Conformity with the Recently Discovered Remains*, p. 10.) Of course, the modern word "mausoleum" (usually a stone building where the bodies of the deceased are entombed aboveground) was named after King Mausolus.

VI The Colossus of Rhodes. The Colossus of Rhodes was a statue of the Greek Titan Helios erected in the island city of Rhodes designed and constructed (with help, of course) by the great Greek sculptor Chares of Lindos between 292 and 280 B.C. Before its destruction and ultimate disappearance, the Colossus of Rhodes purportedly stood more than 107 feet high, making it one of the tallest statues of the ancient world.

Preserved in Greek anthologies (*Anthologia Graeca* 4.171), the following poem is believed to be the original dedication speech for the Colossus:

To you, o Sun, the people of Dorian Rhodes set up this bronze statue reaching to Olympus, when they had pacified the waves of war and crowned their city with the spoils taken from the enemy. Not only over the seas but also on land did they kindle the lovely torch of freedom and independence. For to the descendants of Herakles belongs dominion over sea and land.

After an earthquake in 226 B.C., the Colossus of Rhodes quickly became a colossal wreck. The Colossus lives on, however, because the design (holding a torch and wearing a headdress with pointed rays) was emulated by designer Frédéric Bartholdi for the Statue of Liberty.

VII The Lighthouse of Alexandria. The Lighthouse of Alexandria was a tower built between 280 and 247 B.C. on the island of Pharos at Alexandria, Egypt. Its purpose was more functional than ceremonial: It was a lighthouse, albeit a grand lighthouse, and it was designed to guide sailors into the harbor at nighttime. Pharos was a small island just off the coast of Alexandria, and it was rumored that its inhabitants would destroy any ship that was wrecked off of its coast. Ptolemy I, who assumed the title of king after the death of Alexander the Great in 305 B.C., had the 393- or 450-foot lighthouse built to show that there was a new man on the block. The lighthouse was badly damaged in a series of earthquakes (A.D. 956, 1303, and 1323), and the remains were eventually recycled in 1480 when the sultan of Egypt Qaitbay used them to build a fort.

"FOR FRACTURES OF THE CRANIUM, COBWEBS ARE APPLIED, WITH OIL AND VINEGAR; THE APPLICATION NEVER COMING AWAY TILL A CURE HAS BEEN EFFECTED. COBWEBS ARE GOOD, TOO, FOR STOPPING THE BLEEDING OF WOUNDS MADE IN SHAVING." (PLINY, *NATURAL HISTORY* 29.114.)

STUPID
ANCIENT
HISTORY

Time Passages

Alot of us learned that B.C. is an abbreviation for "Before Christ," so some assumed, incorrectly, that A.D. stood for "After Death." But A.D. is an abbreviation for the Latin *anno Domini*, meaning "in the year of our Lord." It was created by Dionysius Exiguus, a monk born in Scythia Minor around A.D. 500. If A.D. did stand for "After Death," then there would be a thirty-three-year hole in the calendar representing the time Jesus was alive.

TECHNICALLY SPEAKING, A.D. SHOULD APPEAR
BEFORE THE DATE IT QUALIFIES, WHEREAS B.C.
SHOULD ALWAYS FOLLOW THE DATE.

It's the Law

Sometime around 1780 B.C., King Hammurabi of Babylon decided to lay down the law by having his 282 edicts carved into an eight-foot-high column and erected where all his subjects could see it. (No one could claim ignorance of the law after this.) At the top, to make sure everyone knew he was large and in charge, he had the royal artists carve an image of the great king on his palatial throne. The column is referred to as the Code of Hammurabi.

The laws are arranged in orderly groups dealing with property, livestock, agriculture, inheritance rights, and others. There are the standard "eye for an eye" (196) and "tooth for a tooth" (200) decrees, but there is no mention of prison. Punishment is usually death, being thrown in the river, fines, compensation, or having your ear cut off. Strangely enough, there is no listing for the crime of murder, either. An example:

> 2. If anyone brings an accusation against a man, and the accused goes to the river and leaps into the river, if he sinks in the river his accuser shall take possession of his house.

People didn't know how to swim in those days, so if someone was thrown in the river and their body floated back to shore he was innocent; otherwise, case closed.

CC

A CODE TO LIVE BY

The Code of Hammurabi, was, to say the least, very strict—especially if you were of low social standing. Say someone steals a goat. If the goat "belonged to a god" (that is, was stolen from a temple—the tippy-top of the social scale), the thief had to pay thirty times the worth of the goat. If the goat belonged to a "free man"—someone a step up from a regular citizen—the thief had to pay just ten times the amount. If the thief was too poor to pay the fine, he was put to death. Here are two examples of social status punishment from the Code:

202. If anyone strikes the body of a man higher in rank than he, he shall receive sixty blows with an ox whip in public.

203. If a free-born man strikes the body of another free-born man or equal rank, he shall pay one gold mina.

CCI

JOIN THE CLUB

Ishtar, apart from being one of the worst movies ever made, was the Babylonian goddess of war, love, fertility, and sex, and the most powerful goddess in the Mesopotamian religion. In order to be initiated into Ishtar's cult, every female citizen was expected to go to the temple of Ishtar and offer herself for sacred prostitution to any male worshipper who shelled out the required contribution. There was no shame in being one of Ishtar's prostitutes; in fact, it was a very desirable thing because it was considered a sacred means of attaining divine union between mortal and goddess. The English writer Sir James Frazer, in his book *The Golden Bough: A Study in Magic and Religion* (1890), mentions the unfortunate wallflowers who didn't make the cut: "The sacred precinct [Ishtar's temple] was crowded with women waiting to observe the custom. Some of them had to wait there for years."

CCII

"A SURGEON SHOULD BE FAIRLY YOUNG, WITH STRONG AND STEADY HANDS, AMBIDEXTROUS, WITH GOOD EYESIGHT, EAGER TO CURE HIS PATIENT, BUT DETACHED ENOUGH NOT TO WANT TO HURRY OR TO CUT LESS THAN IS NECESSARY. HE HAS TO PERFORM HIS TASK AS IF THE PATIENT'S SCREAMS HAD NO EFFECT ON HIM." (CELSUS, *ON MEDICINE* 7.)

BEARING FALSE WITNESS IV

"The lion shall lie down with the lamb." This nonbiblical phrase was taken from Isaiah 11:6 and was drastically shortened and altered, probably because the playful alliteration of "lion" and "lamb" makes it more singsongy. The actual quote is "The wolf also shall dwell with the lamb, and the leopard shall lie down with the kid; and the calf and the young lion and the fatling together; and a little child shall lead them." (Isaiah 11:6 NIV.)

"Spare the rod, spoil the child." This exact Bible verse is nowhere in the Bible, but there are many similar Bible verses that say essentially the same thing. "Whoever spares the rod hates their children, but the one who loves their children is careful to discipline them." (Proverbs 13:24 NIV. See also Proverbs 22:15; 23:13-14; 29:15—King Solomon certainly liked whipping kids, didn't he?) The phrase as we have come to know it probably came from Samuel Butler, in his satirical poem *Hudibras*, published in 1662:

> Love is a Boy,
> by Poets styl'd,
> Then Spare the Rod,
> and spill [spoil] the Child.

STUPID
ANCIENT
HISTORY

Splish, Splash, I Was Takin' a Bath

A bath in ancient Rome wasn't your typical tub or even modern Jacuzzi. These structures were palatial and enormously luxurious. Usually made of marble and tile and decorated with mosaics, some had gardens, libraries, and even lecture halls—they weren't the one-room structures of modern days. In most cases they were named for the emperors who built them: the baths of Caracalla, for instance, covered nearly twenty-eight acres. Ancient Rome had as many as 952 public baths: small baths (*balneum*) held about three people, and the larger baths were called *thermae* (the largest of these, the Baths of Diocletian, could hold up to three thousand bathers).

Seneca (*Letter* 56.1–2) described the baths as an incredibly noisy place: "Conjure up in your imagination all the sounds that make one hate one's ears." Seneca complained about the people making noise while exercising, the loud mouth swimmer, people getting a massage, and to top it all off, "Now add the mingled cries of the drink peddler and the sellers of sausages, pastries, and hot fare, each hawking his own wares with his own particular peal." And my personal favorite bothersome noise, "the skinny armpit-hair plucker whose cries are shrill so as to draw people's attention."

TO PREVENT BLISTERS ON A
LONG JOURNEY CATO THE
ELDER RECOMMENDED PUTTING
A SPRIG OF WORMWOOD
IN ONE'S RECTUM. (CATO,
ON FARMING 159.)

GO SOAK YOUR HEAD

During the time of Julius Caesar (100–44 B.C.) men and women weren't allowed at the baths at the same time—they were assigned a separate schedule. Eventually, however, mixed bathing was allowed. But a few ground rules had to be laid down first—the Romans loved their law. The first rule was "Don't stare" and the second was "Behave as though fully dressed." As the Roman Empire declined, the morals in the baths declined as well, and they were occasionally used for orgies and licentious behavior. It's argued by some historians and sociologists that early Christian societies frowned upon nudity and bathing. For me, the best part about the baths, apart from the nudity, is that no children were allowed.

THE GREEK HISTORIAN
POLYBIUS (200–118 B.C.) AND
GENERAL PUBLIUS CORNELIUS
SCIPIO AEMILIANUS AFRICANUS
NUMANTINUS (185–129 B.C.),
WHO DESTROYED CARTHAGE
IN 146 B.C., REPORTEDLY SAW
MAN-EATING LIONS BEING
CRUCIFIED AS A WARNING AND
DETERRENT TO OTHER LIONS.
(PLINY, *NATURAL HISTORY* 8.47.)

MUMMY MILL

S. J. Wolfe, lecturer, senior cataloger, and serials specialist at the American Antiquarian Society, in Worcester, Massachusetts, says that ground mummified bodies were used to produce a brown pigment, still referred to as "mummy brown" or "Egyptian brown." ("I. Augustus Stanwood Had a Paper Mill in Maine," Kennebec Historical Society Meeting, Christ Church, Gardiner, Maine, July 19, 2006.) Other mummy-made products included aromatic oils, such as olibanum and ambergris, which, according to Nicholson Baker, were made into machine oils and soaps by distilling the mummified bodies. (Nicholson Baker, "Virgin Mummies," *Double Fold: Libraries and the Assault on Paper,* p. 59.)

"PUTTING GOAT DUNG IN THEIR DIAPERS
SOOTHES HYPERACTIVE CHILDREN, ESPECIALLY
GIRLS." (PLINY, *NATURAL HISTORY* 28.259.)

BETTER THAN A
SHARP STICK IN THE EYE?

After using the public latrines (it seems like the Romans liked to do everything in public), a citizen of Rome looked for the bucket—or in some cases a trough right in front of the toilet—which held saltwater and a long stick with a sea sponge attached to one end. Without getting too graphic, the person would use the sponge to clean himself or herself after defecating and then rinse the sponge and return it for the next patron's use. If your thoughts were elsewhere, or if you were engaged in a lively conversation, you might carelessly use the stick incorrectly. This is said to be the origin of the phrase "getting the wrong end of the stick."

WHEN KING PYRRHUS OF EPIRUS (318–272 B.C.) DIED AND WAS CREMATED, EVERY PART OF HIS BODY TURNED TO ASH EXCEPT THE BIG TOE ON HIS RIGHT FOOT. IT WAS HONORED AS SACRED AND KEPT IN A CASKET IN A TEMPLE. ACCORDING TO PLINY THE ELDER, AILMENTS OF THE SPLEEN COULD BE CURED BY CONTACT WITH PYRRHUS'S BIG TOE. (PLINY, *NATURAL HISTORY* 7.20.)

DON'T GET CARRIED AWAY

Romano-Jewish historian Titus Flavius Josephus (A.D. 37–100) wrote extensively about the history of Judaism, most notably in his books *The Jewish War* and *Antiquities of the Jews*. He reported that there were different subgroups within ancient Judaism, including the Pharisees, the Sadducees, and the Essenes, and that there was a "fourth sect." (Josephus, *Antiquity of the Jews* 18.) The Zealots were founded by Judas of Galilee, mentioned in the Bible in Acts 5:37 (but not *that* Judas) and Zadok the Pharisee in the year A.D. 6. They were a violent, nationalistic revolutionary party opposed to the Romans. At the time, the term "zealot" meant one who is zealous on behalf of God, from the Greek *zelotes*, meaning "emulator, zealous admirer, or follower." But the Zealots got out of hand and are considered by many to be one of the first examples of the use of terrorism by Jews. (Mark Burgess, "A Brief History of Terrorism.") A splinter group of the Zealots were the Sicarii, who concealed *sicae*, or small daggers, under their cloaks and would maim and kill Romans in broad daylight. It is from the Zealots that we get the current meaning of "zealot" as a fanatical partisan or someone carried away by zeal.

PAGING DR. FREUD

Issued long before Sigmund Freud described the controversial "Oedipus complex"—a psychoanalytic theory pertaining to a boy's desire to sexually possess his mother—was second-century diviner Artemidorus Daldianus's five-volume book, *Oneirocritica* (*The Interpretation of Dreams*). Here's how he analyzes a man dreaming about his mother:

> But for a man who is involved in a lawsuit over land rights, for a man who wants to purchase land, and for a man who would like to farm land, it is good to have intercourse [in his dreams] with one's dead mother. Some people say that it indicates bad luck only for farmers. For they will cast their seeds down into, as it were, dead land. That is, it will bear no fruit. In my opinion, this does not seem to be the case at all unless, of course, the person dreams that he repents or is distressed by the intercourse. (Artemidorus Daldianus, *Oneirocritica* 1.1.79.)

CCXIII

NO TURNING BACK NOW

The idiom "crossing the Rubicon" means to pass a point of no return. But where did the phrase come from? The Rubicon is actually a shallow river in northeastern Italy and derived its name from the Latin adjective *rubeus*, meaning "red" (because the red mud deposits have colored the water). In early 49 B.C., Julius Caesar led one legion, the Legio XIII Gemina, over the Rubicon, which was the border of another Roman province. This was considered an act of insurrection, making armed conflict inevitable. The Roman Republic was divided into several provinces, and the leader of one wasn't allowed in another. So by deciding to cross the Rubicon, Caesar knew full well he had passed the point of no return. According to the historian Suetonius, upon crossing, Caesar uttered the famous phrase "*ālea iacta est*"—"the die has been cast." (Suetonius *Lives of the Caesars* "Divus Julius" 32.) Caesar was never punished for the crime because his ultimate victory in the Great Roman Civil War eventually led to him becoming dictator.

IN ORDER TO ENSURE THAT INFANTS GROW UP STRONG AND HEALTHY, CATO THE ELDER SUGGESTED THAT THE PARENTS WASH THE BABY IN THE URINE OF SOMEONE WHO HAS BEEN LIVING ON A DIET OF CABBAGE. (*ON FARMING* 157.10.)

MESSAGES
FROM THE PAST IX

Graffiti from Pompeii, collected and recorded in the *Corpus Inscriptionum Latinarum*. The number after the location in parentheses is the catalog number of the inscription (not the date) in volume 4:

- (Triclinium of a house) 5251: "Restitutus has deceived many girls."

- Nuceria Necropolis (on a tomb) 10231: "Serena hates Isidorus."

- Herculaneum (bar/inn joined to the maritime baths) 10675: "Two friends were here. While they were, they had bad service in every way from a guy named Epaphroditus. They threw him out and spent 105 and half *sestertii* most agreeably on whores."

- Herculaneum (bar/inn joined to the maritime baths) 10677: "Apelles the chamberlain with Dexter, a slave of Caesar, ate here most agreeably and had a screw at the same time."

- Herculaneum (bar/inn joined to the maritime baths) 10678: "Apelles Mus and his brother Dexter each pleasurably had sex with two girls twice."

- Herculaneum (on a water distribution tower) 10488: "Anyone who wants to defecate in this place is advised to move along. If you act contrary to this warning, you will have to pay a penalty. Children must pay [number missing] silver coins. Slaves will be beaten on their behinds."

SAUCY SAUSAGE

Although a lot of people assume that the word "sausage" is of German origin, since Germans are known worldwide for their love of sausage, it's actually a Latin word. "Sausage" comes from the Latin *salsus*, meaning "salted," because that's how it's cured. The first recorded reference was in Homer's *Odyssey* (eighth century B.C.):

> "A man beside a great fire has filled a sausage with fat and blood, and turns it this way and that and is eager to get it quickly roasted."

Epicharmus wrote a comedy titled *Orya* (*The Sausage*) in about 500 B.C., and Aristophanes's play *The Knights* (424 B.C.) is about a sausage vendor who is elected leader. The Germans didn't come around until much later, so there's no way they were responsible for the word "sausage." It would have been wonderfully ironic if the name "sausage" had been invented by the Franks, wouldn't it?

THE ROMAN GENERAL AND
STATESMAN LUCIUS CORNELIUS
SULLA FELIX (138–78 B.C.)—HIS
FRIENDS JUST CALLED HIM SULLA—
HAD THE RARE DISTINCTION OF
HOLDING THE OFFICE OF CONSUL
TWICE. SULLA HAD SOME 1,500
NOBLES EXECUTED FOR FEAR THAT
THEY WERE ACTING AGAINST HIM.
ONE PUBLIUS SULPICIUS RUFUS WAS
KILLED BY SULLA'S ORDERS IN THE
80S B.C. THE SLAVE WHO BETRAYED
HIM WAS GIVEN HIS FREEDOM
AS A REWARD—BUT WAS THEN
THROWN OVER A CLIFF FOR THE
CRIME OF BETRAYING HIS MASTER.
(LIVY, *HISTORY OF ROME* 77.)

THE TERRIBLE TUBE MEAT

A special spiced sausage made with pork, pine nuts, and pepper was a favorite dish at the ancient Roman festival of Februa, the festival of ritual purification, which was later incorporated into the festival of Lupercalia, a celebration of the Roman god of flocks. These traditions date to pre-Roman times and were very much part of the culture in early Rome. Things usually got out of hand during these celebrations, and an orgy would routinely break out. Early Christians disapproved, and when Christian emperor Constantine the Great came into power in A.D. 324, he thought he could appease the Christians by banning not the festival but the sausage. This quickly created a black market in sausages, which lasted several years until Constantine lifted the sausage ban.

CCXIX

ORATOR SIMILE TANTUM VERI PETIT . . . NON ENIM BONA CONSCIENTIA SED VICTORIA LITIGANTIS EST PRAEMIUM: "A LAWYER AIMS ONLY FOR A SEMBLANCE OF THE TRUTH . . . FOR A LITIGANT'S REWARD IS A FAVORABLE RULING, NOT A GOOD CONSCIENCE." (QUINTILIAN, *EDUCATION OF THE ORATOR* 2.15.32.)

STUPID
ANCIENT
HISTORY

That Time of the Month

The Roman month Februarius (the modern February) is named for the Februa festival, which occurred on the thirteenth to fifteenth days of this Roman month. Later, a Roman god Februus personified both the month and purification, and is named for them. There is no connection between the Februa festival and Saint Valentine's Day, other than they occurred at the same time of the month.

THE CELEBRATION OF SAINT VALENTINE,
AND SAINT VALENTINE'S DAY, DIDN'T HAVE
ANY ROMANTIC CONNOTATIONS UNTIL
GEOFFREY CHAUCER WROTE POETRY ABOUT
"VALENTINES" IN THE FOURTEENTH CENTURY.

CELEBRATE GOOD TIMES, COME ON!

To celebrate his victory over the Roman general Pompey in 49 B.C., Julius Caesar gave a banquet, and in traditional Roman style it was a doozy. Plutarch (A.D. 46–120) records it thus:

> After the triumphs, he distributed rewards to his soldiers, and treated the people with feasting and shows. He entertained the whole people together at one feast, where twenty-two thousand dining couches were laid out; and he made a display of gladiators, and of battles by sea, in honor, as he said, of his daughter Julia, though she had been long since dead. When these shows were over, an account [census] was taken of the people, who, from three hundred and twenty thousand, were now reduced to one hundred and fifty thousand. So great a waste had the civil war made in Rome alone, not to mention what the other parts of Italy and the provinces suffered. (Plutarch, *Life of Julius Caesar* 4.55.)

THE WALL OF SHAME

The Romans were known to draw sexualized caricatures with abnormally large penises, and I mean *abnormally large*. The character became such a part of Roman graffiti that they gave it a name, *sopio* (which is contemporarily translated as "penis"). It appears in the poems of Gaius Valerius Catullus (*Catullus* 37): *Frontem tabernae sopionibus scribam* ("I will draw *sopios* on the front of the tavern") and in graffiti from Pompeii: *Ut merdas edatis, qui scripseras sopionis* ("Whoever drew *sopios*, let him eat sh!t!"). The grammarian Sacerdos told about an insult directed at Pompey: *Quem non pudet et rubet, non est homo, sed sopio* ("Whoever is not ashamed and blushes is not a man, but a *sopio*.") (J. N. Adams, *The Latin Sexual Vocabulary*, p. 64.)

"DESPITE THE NORMAL UPROAR IN THE JULIAN BASILICA WHEN ALL FOUR COURTS WERE IN SESSION CONCURRENTLY, AN EXCEPTIONALLY LOUD-VOICED ORATOR NAMED TRACHALUS COULD MAKE HIMSELF HEARD AND UNDERSTOOD SO EFFECTIVELY THAT, MUCH TO THE ANNOYANCE OF THE OTHER LAWYERS IN THE COURT WHERE HE WAS SPEAKING, EVEN THE AUDIENCE AT THE OTHER THREE TRIALS APPLAUDED HIM." (QUINTILIAN, *EDUCATION OF THE ORATOR* 12.5.6.)

THOSE PEARLY WHITES

The ancient Greeks cherished having white teeth (about as much as modern-day Westerners do), especially among aristocratic men. They tried everything—emery, granulated alabaster, pumice, talcum, powdered coral, and iron rust—on their teeth. Those abrasives did the trick for a while until they wore off the enamel, exposed the nerves, and left the person in extreme agony. The great Greek physician Hippocrates (460–370 B.C.) suggested a concoction consisting of three mice and a burned rabbit's head to brush with. The Romans brushed their teeth with powders made from ground antlers, hooves, crabs, eggshells, and lizard livers.

"THE LAWS ARE LIKE SPIDERS' WEBS: JUST AS SPIDERS' WEBS CATCH THE WEAKER CREATURES BUT LET THE STRONGER ONES THROUGH, SO THE HUMBLE AND POOR ARE RESTRICTED BY THE LAWS, BUT THE RIGHT AND POWERFUL ARE NOT BOUND BY THEM." (VALERIUS MAXIMUS, *MEMORABLE DEEDS AND SAYINGS* 7.2.14.)

WORM HOLE THEORY

In ancient times, before mankind understood the physiology of the human body, many people thought that a toothache was caused by a tooth worm. This tooth-worm theory can be traced back to Mesopotamia (modern-day Iraq) from a Sumerian text dated to 5000 B.C., and this belief persisted until the eighteenth century. To stop this nasty little critter from boring holes in your teeth, the Aztecs of Mexico recommended chewing on hot chili. In Scotland, the cure was to wrap a caterpillar in red cloth and place it under the aching tooth. Indian surgeon Vagbhata, who lived around 650 A.D., had a more aggressive approach: He advised filling the tooth cavity with wax and burning it with a hot poker. ("History of Dentistry: Ancient Origins," American Dental Association.)

CORRUPTISSIMA RE PUBLICA PLURIMAE LEGES:
"MOST LAWS ARE PASSED WHEN THE STATE
IS MOST CORRUPT." (TACITUS, *ANNALS* 3.27.)
MY, HOW THINGS DON'T CHANGE.

ANCIENT CHINESE SECRET

An ancient Chinese cure for toothaches was a mix of garlic, horseradish, and human milk, which was then made into a paste. That's certainly not as strange as some of the remedies of ancient times. But then the paste was rolled into pills and stuck up the patient's nostril on the side opposite the toothache. Of course, the Chinese also discovered, around 2700 B.C., the curative and pain-relieving effects of acupuncture to combat toothache pain. They must have been doing something right, because human remains have been found from as early as A.D. 659 with teeth that had been drilled and filled with a mixture of silver, tin, and mercury—something very close to the silver amalgam still used today.

CCXXVIII

NEC BONUM NEC MALUM VAGINA GLADIUM FACIT DOESN'T MEAN WHAT YOU THINK IT MIGHT MEAN. IT TRANSLATES TO "A SCABBARD MAKES A SWORD NEITHER GOOD NOR BAD." (SENECA, *LETTERS* 92.13.)

THE WISDOM OF TOOTH CURES

"Erigeron is called by our people *senecio*. It is said that if a person, after tracing around this plant with an implement of iron, takes it up and touches the tooth affected with it three times, taking care to spit each time on the ground, and then replaces it in the same spot, so as to take root again, he will never experience any further pain in that tooth." (Pliny, *Natural History* 25.106.)

CCXXX

PLINY THE ELDER ALSO DESCRIBED SEVERAL OTHER UNIQUE APPROACHES TO CURING DENTAL PAIN IN HIS BOOK, *NATURAL HISTORY*: "THE TEETH OF THE HYENA ARE USEFUL FOR THE CURE OF TOOTH-ACHE." "TO STOP TOOTHACHE BITE ON A PIECE OF WOOD FROM A TREE STRUCK BY LIGHTNING." OR, "TOUCH THE TOOTH WITH THE FRONTAL BONE OF A LIZARD TAKEN DURING THE FULL MOON." (PLINY, *NATURAL HISTORY* 28.26, 28.12, 30.8.)

Ain't That the Tooth

"[Greek philosopher] Xenocrates [396–314 B.C.] gives the name of *gallidraga* to a plant which resembles the leucanthus and grows in the marshes. It is a prickly plant, with a tall, ferulaceous stem, surmounted with a head somewhat similar to an egg in appearance. When this head is growing, in summer, small worms, he says, are generated, which are put away in a box for keeping, and are attached as an amulet, with bread, to the arm on the side on which toothache is felt; indeed it is quite wonderful, he says, how soon the pain is removed. These worms, however, are of no use after the end of a year, or in cases where they have been allowed to touch the ground." (Pliny, *Natural History* 28.62.)

"THE MOST EFFECTUAL REMEDY FOR TOOTHACHE IS TO SCARIFY [CUT] THE GUMS WITH THE TOOTH OF A MAN WHO HAS DIED A VIOLENT DEATH." (PLINY, *NATURAL HISTORY* 28.2A.)

FOUR OUT OF FIVE DENTISTS AGREE

"But to proceed with the remedies for toothache—the magicians tell us that it may be cured by using the ashes of the head of a dog that has died in a state of madness. The head, however, must be burnt without the flesh, and the ashes injected with oil of Cyprus into the ear on the side affected." Or "a mouse is to be eaten twice a month, as a preventive of toothache. Earthworms, boiled in oil and injected into the ear on the side affected, afford considerable relief." (Pliny, *Natural History* 30.8.)

CCXXXIII

THE VINDOLANDA TABLETS ARE THOUSANDS OF THIN, POSTCARD-SIZED WOODEN LEAF TABLETS FOUND IN 1973 AT THE ROMAN FORT IN VINDOLANDA, NEAR HADRIAN'S WALL—THEY ARE "THE OLDEST SURVIVING HANDWRITTEN DOCUMENTS IN BRITAIN." BUT BASICALLY, THEY'RE JUST LETTERS TO SOLDIERS FROM FAMILY AND FRIENDS, LIKE THIS SIMPLE NOTE REMINDING US THOUSANDS OF YEARS LATER THAT PEOPLE ARE JUST PEOPLE. A CONCERNED PARENT OR SPOUSE WRITES: "I HAVE SENT YOU [TWO] PAIRS OF SOCKS, TWO PAIRS OF SANDALS, TWO PAIRS OF UNDERPANTS." (TABLET 346.)

THE GODS MUST BE CRAZY

Here is a partial list of some rather unusual Roman gods:

- Bubona, goddess of cattle

- Cloacina, goddess who presided over the system of sewers in Rome

- Devera, goddess who ruled over the brooms used to purify temples in preparation for various worship services

- Feronia, rural goddess of woods and fountains

- Forculus, a god who protected doors

- Hostilina, goddess who ensured that ears of corn developed evenly

- Mellona, goddess of bees and beekeeping

- Nodutus, god who made knots in stalks of wheat

- Portunes, god of keys, doors, and livestock

- Potina, goddess of children's drinks

- Puta, goddess of pruning vines and bushes

- Sterquilinus, god of fertilizer

- Verminus, god of cattle worms

PAIN, PAIN, GO AWAY

The ancient Greeks probably used opium as a painkiller for dental procedures. The Romans, however, used to apply the pickled root of a chrysanthemum to gums to deaden pain. It worked to an extent, but it had a pretty bad side effect: It loosened and destroyed the membrane holding the tooth in place. So if a patient continued to have trouble with a particular tooth, several treatments of pickled chrysanthemum eventually caused the tooth to fall out (which, I guess, got rid of the tooth problem). Another popular Roman painkilling potion was a paste made from opium, celandine (known for its analgesic properties), and saffron. So what's so weird about this? Nothing, until you find out that the Romans then added ground lizards, bone marrow, and human fat. A final painkilling remedy used in ancient Roman times was to apply pressure to the carotid arteries in the neck, which would slow blood flow and induce unconsciousness (and sometimes death).

THE EMPEROR HADRIAN RULED THAT ANY SOLDIER WHO ATTEMPTED SUICIDE BECAUSE OF BOREDOM WITH LIFE (*TAEDIUM VITAE*) SHOULD BE DISHONORABLY DISCHARGED. (*JUSTINIAN'S DIGEST* 49.16.6.7.)

DRILL, BABY, DRILL

Hesi-Re (ca. 2600 B.C.) is the first recorded "dentist" in history. On his tombstone is engraved "Doctor of the Tooth." Some of the procedures used in ancient Egypt are still used today, primarily drilling. Unfortunately back then the drilling probably didn't work. You see, instead of drilling out the decayed part of the tooth, dentists would, judging from various mummies who had dental care, drill into the jawbone beneath the aching tooth. The theory is that they did this in an attempt to relieve pressure.

AULUS CORNELIUS CELSUS
(25 B.C.–A.D. 50) SUGGESTED IN
HIS BOOK *DE MEDICINA* THAT
A PATIENT SUFFERING FROM
BLEEDING GUMS SHOULD
CHEW UNRIPE PEARS AND
ALLOW THE JUICE TO RUN
INTO THE CREVICES OF THE
TEETH (I'M CRINGING, TOO).
IF THAT PROCEDURE WAS
UNSUCCESSFUL, CELSUS
RECOMMENDED ANOTHER
APPROACH: CAUTERIZING
THE INFECTED GUMS
WITH A RED-HOT IRON.

LITTLE LEGIONS

The old sayings "There's strength in numbers" and "the more the merrier" were beliefs that could be ascribed to ancient Roman times. At its zenith (around A.D. 200–250), the territory under control of the Roman Empire was close to the size of the contiguous United States today. Census records show that the population at that time was more than 100 million, with the city of Rome at one million. Gaius Julius Caesar Augustus (63 B.C.–A.D. 14), the first emperor of the Roman Empire, wanted more Roman citizens and passed legislation to encourage marriage and childbearing. The unmarried and the childless suffered political and financial penalties while those with three or more children received special privileges. Childless wives were forbidden to ride in litters or to wear jewelry.

CCXL

"AS WELL AS THEIR OTHER EQUIPMENT, ROMAN SOLDIERS WEAR AS A DECORATION ON THEIR HELMETS A CIRCLE OF FEATHERS WITH THREE PURPLE OR BLACK PLUMES SET STRAIGHT UP ABOUT ONE AND A HALF FEET. WITH THIS THEY APPEAR TWICE THEIR ACTUAL HEIGHT AND ARE A FEARSOME SIGHT, INTIMIDATING TO THE ENEMY." (POLYBIUS, *HISTORIES* 6.23.) WE KNOW WHAT POLYBIUS WAS TRYING TO SAY BUT ROMAN SOLDIERS WERE MORE THAN EIGHTEEN INCHES TALL.

STUPID
ANCIENT
HISTORY

THERE'S SOMETHING FISHY IN ROME

In most restaurants today, you can find ketchup, mustard, vinegar, and hot sauce as condiments on your table. But the Roman Empire's favorite condiment was garum, a fermented fish sauce. To prepare garum one would crush the innards of various fishes such as mackerel, tuna, eel, and others, and then ferment them in brine for several weeks, or up to three months. The smell of the fermenting garum was so disgusting that a law was passed forcing production to the outskirts of town. (Robert I. Curtis, "Salted Fish Products in Ancient Medicine," *Journal of the History of Medicine and Allied Sciences* 39, no. 4 [1984]: 430–45.) The Romans used it on everything, and, according to Pliny the Elder, it could be diluted to the "color of honey wine and drunk." (Pliny, *Natural History* 13.93.) Although it sounds pretty gross and smelled like rotten fish, it was actually very nutritious—high in protein and amino acids and a good source of B vitamins.

CCXLII

IN NAME ONLY

The expression "Barbarians at the gate" was literally true in A.D. 408 when the Gothic king Alaric I had surrounded the eastern Roman Empire. Being barbarians, of course, they attacked the city, madly killing, plundering, and raping anything they could get their hands on, right? No, they waited patiently outside. Having cut off all supplies in and out of Rome, they just sat there until the Romans ran out of food. Eventually two brave Roman delegates cautiously went outside to meet the horrible barbarian Alaric, sure that they would be eviscerated and eaten (because that's what barbarians do). They were surprised when they met the very intelligent, very cordial leader. They asked him about a peace treaty. Alaric said he and his forces would leave if the Romans paid them in gold and silver and released to his care all the barbarian slaves.

"What will you leave us?" asked the delegates.

"Your lives," Alaric replied.

Both parties agreed to the deal and soon Rome's gates were opened and out poured thirty thousand barbarian slaves. So what did Alaric do next, owing to the fact that he now had thirty thousand more potential forces? Attack anyway and sack the city? No, he did what he said he would; he took the slaves and moved his troops out of Roman territory. The barbarian Alaric acted with more restraint and reason than any "civilized" army of the time would have used.

STICKS AND STONES . . .

Invented by the ancient Greeks (like most things, apparently), the term "barbarian" (Greek *barbaoi*) at that time simply referred to anyone who was not Greek, did not speak Greek, did not act Greek, and did not live in Greece—primarily the Etruscans, Carthaginians, Persians, and Egyptians. Modern use of the word "barbarian" could certainly not be equated with the cultures of Persia and Egypt; the meaning has changed. Linguistic scholars are still uncertain as to how the term "barbarian" originated, but one of the more accepted theories is that it came from mocking the language of foreigners. To the undiscerning Greek ear, it might sound as if someone speaking a foreign tongue was saying "bar-bar-bar" and hence the term "barbarian." In a turn of phrase, when the Romans picked up the term, they applied it to their enemies: the tribes of northern Europe (Goths, Visigoths, Ostrogoths, Vandals, Huns, and so forth).

THE FEMALE NAME "BARBARA" ORIGINALLY
MEANT "A BARBARIAN WOMAN" AND WAS
MORE THAN LIKELY A DEROGATORY WORD.

DOING A DOUBLE TAKE

When people, even today, hear the word "Goth," when related to ancient times, they think of pagan barbarians—but they weren't. Within a few generations of the Goths' appearance on the borders of the Roman Empire in a.d. 238, the main Gothic religion was Christianity. Artifacts such as Gothic coins dating from A.D. 311 are embossed with the Christian cross, and one of their members, a Gothic bishop by the name of Theophilus Gothiae, was present at the Council of Nicaea in A.D. 325. So, contrary to popular belief, the Goths, who were called barbarians, were predominantly Christian, and the great Roman Empire was predominantly composed of pagans.

CCXLV

THE PARTHIAN CAVALRY WERE
NOTORIOUS FOR THEIR SKILL IN
ARCHERY. AT THE BATTLE OF CARRHAE
IN 53 B.C. (CONSIDERED BY MANY
HISTORIANS TO BE THE ONLY GREAT
BATTLE DECIDED BY ARCHERY), THEY
MASSACRED NOT ONLY THE LEGION'S
LEADER, MARCUS LICINIUS CRASSUS
(115–53 B.C.), BUT ALSO HIS ENTIRE ARMY.
THE ARCHERS WERE PARTICULARLY
NOTED FOR THEIR TRICK OF SHOOTING
BACKWARD WHILE IN FULL RETREAT,
WHICH GAVE RISE TO THE PHRASE
"PARTHIAN SHOT," WHICH EVOLVED
INTO THE IDIOM "PARTING SHOT."

ACTS TO DIE FOR III

The Bible and the Torah are filled with crimes worthy of death. If you agree with one you're supposed to agree with them all. Here's a sampling of deadly acts:

- "If a man commits adultery with another man's wife—with the wife of his neighbor—both the adulterer and the adulteress must be put to death." (Leviticus 20:10 NIV.)

- "If a man has sexual relations with his father's wife, he has dishonored his father. Both the man and the woman must be put to death; their blood will be on their own heads." (Leviticus 20:11 NIV.)

- "If a man has sexual relations with his daughter-in-law, both of them are to be put to death." (Leviticus 20:12 NIV.)

- "If a man also lie with mankind, as he lieth with a woman, both of them have committed an abomination: they shall surely be put to death; their blood shall be upon them." (Leviticus 20:13 KJV.)

- "If a man marries both a woman and her mother, it is wicked. Both he and they must be burned in the fire, so that no wickedness will be among you." (Leviticus 20:14 NIV.)

- If a man or woman has sex with an animal, both human and animal must be killed. (Leviticus 20:15–16.)

Do's and Don'ts of the Torah

Apart from all the acts that carry a death penalty, there are some laws that don't make a lot of sense for modern man:

- Don't let cattle graze with other kinds of cattle. (Leviticus 19:19.)

- Don't have a variety of crops on the same field. (Leviticus 19:19.)

- Don't wear clothes made of more than one fabric. (Leviticus 19:19.)

- Don't cut your hair nor shave. (Leviticus 19:27.)

- If a man has sex with a woman on her period, they are both to be "cut off from among their people." (Leviticus 20:18 KJV.)

"AS A COUNTERMEASURE TO ASSAULT BY A BATTERING RAM, A SACK FILLED WITH STRAW IS LET DOWN TO THE POINT OF IMPACT, FOR THE BLOWS OF THE BATTERING RAM ARE DEADENED BY THE SOFT BILLOWING SACK." (SAINT ISIDORE, *ETYMOLOGIES* 18.11.)

HISTORICAL HYSTERIA

It was a long-standing belief, originating with the Greek philosopher Plato (423 B.C.–348 B.C.) that a woman's emotional problems could be blamed on her own womb. The Greek word for womb is *hystera* and from that root we get the words "hysterectomy" (removal of the uterus) as well as the word "hysteria" (unmanageable emotional excesses), and "hysterical." In ancient times the womb was so mysterious that it was thought to be an animal living inside the woman's body. According to celebrated Greek physician Aretaeus (first century A.D.):

> In the middle of the flanks of women lies the womb, a female viscus, closely resembling an animal; for it is moved of itself hither and thither in the flanks, also upwards in a direct line to below the cartilage of the thorax and also obliquely to the right or to the left, either to the liver or spleen; and it likewise is subject to falling downward, and, in a word, it is altogether erratic. It delights, also, in fragrant smells, and advances towards them; and it has an aversion to fetid smells, and flees from them; and on the whole the womb is like an animal within an animal. (*Of Aretaeus, the Cappadocian, On the Causes and Symptoms of Acute Disease* 2.11 "On Hysterical Suffocation.")

I MIGHT NOT KNOW ART
BUT I KNOW WHAT I LIKE

In book 2, chapter 3, of *Varia historia* (*Various Histories*), by Claudius Aelianus, entitled "Of Alexander Not Giving Due Commendations of a Picture," Aelian relates the story of Alexander the Great getting a lesson in art appreciation: "Alexander [the Great] beholding his own Picture at Ephesus drawn by Apelles, did not give it such praise as it deserved; but a Horse which was brought in neighed to the painted horse, as if it had been a true one. King, said Apelles, this Horse seems to understand painting much better than you." (Aelian, *Varia historia* 2.3.)

CCL

IN THE WAR WITH MITHRIDATES
THE GREAT IN THE EARLY FIRST
CENTURY B.C., THE ARMY OF
LUCIUS LICINIUS LUCULLUS
(117–56 B.C.) WAS OBSTRUCTED
IN ITS ATTEMPTS TO
TUNNEL UNDER THE CITY
OF THEMISCYRA WHEN
THE INHABITANTS DROVE
BEARS, OTHER WILD
ANIMALS, AND SWARMS OF
BEES INTO THE TUNNELS.

HIS NICKNAME WAS NICK

The famous Greek philosopher Plato was a fraud: "Plato" wasn't his real name; it was a nickname. Plato's real name was Aristocles, son of Ariston, according to Alexander of Miletus (quoted by Diogenes Laërtius in his *Lives and Doctrines of Eminent Philosophers* 3.4). Diogenes goes on to say that the nickname "Plato" was bestowed upon him by Ariston of Argos, a wrestler and Plato's gymnastics teacher, "because of his robust figure." The Greek word *platus* means "wide, broad, broad-shouldered, widespread."

ANOTHER THEORY SAYS PLATO GOT HIS
NICKNAME BECAUSE OF THE BROAD AND
WIDE SHAPE OF HIS FOREHEAD.